Po Chung and Roger Bowie
DHL

Po Chung and Roger Bowie

DHL

From Startup to Global Upstart

ISBN 978-1-5015-1592-7
e-ISBN (PDF) 978-1-5015-0755-7
e-ISBN (EPUB) 978-1-5015-0744-1

Library of Congress Cataloging-in-Publication Data
A CIP catalog record for this book has been applied for at the Library of Congress.

Bibliographic information published by the Deutsche Nationalbibliothek
The Deutsche Nationalbibliothek lists this publication in the Deutsche Nationalbibliografie;
detailed bibliographic data are available on the Internet at http://dnb.dnb.de.

© 2018 Po Chung and Roger Bowie
Published by Walter de Gruyter Inc., Boston/Berlin
Printing and binding: Nomos Verlagsgesellschaft mbH & Co. KG
♾ Printed on acid-free paper
Printed in Germany

www.degruyter.com

Acknowledgments

Po Chung:

A very special tribute to three special persons who contributed to the success, wealth and significance of my DHL journey: the late Adrian Dalsey, the late Larry Hillblom and the late Robert Lynn.

My thanks to Roger Bowie who agreed to co-author this book and for his dedicated commitment to the completion of this book over the past 18 months.

I am grateful to Ken Allen and his team; without his endorsement, we would not have had the opportunity to create the last chapter.

I also extend my gratitude to my old DHL team: David Allen, Bill Robinson and Bill Walden as well as K W Bae, Paul Chan, Rod Feliciano, Neil Ferguson, John Kerr, Pat Lupo, Bill Robinson, Ken Sato, Vivian Tsang, Andy Tseng and Bruce Walker.

I am also thankful to Jeff Pepper and his team at De Gruyter for helping this book see the light of day.

Last but not the least, my lasting gratitude to my dearest wife, Helen, and my three daughters, Yana, Anca and Yangie who always stand by me through the ups and downs of my leadership entrepreneurial journey.

Many thanks to you all.

Roger Bowie:

This has been a labor of love. I had my last days of employment with DHL in May 1995, which coincidentally was exactly the time Larry died in a plane crash off Saipan. Revisiting and reliving those early DHL days has felt like I never left, and the intervening years have just been a holiday.

Many people have helped with the book, so there are many people to thank.

First and foremost, my collaborator and partner in this project, Po Chung, who called me up one day and asked if I could help. Once I got started, Po asked me also to finish it, and so a big vote of thanks to Po, not just for his memory and insights, but for entrusting co-authorship to me.

Thanks also to Po's team in Hong Kong, and specifically Fanny Sze, Shela Chan and Kingsley Smith.

To those DHL Pioneers who provided information, anecdotes, early feedback and encouragement, thank you: Ross Allen, Alec Ang, Geoff Cruikshanks, Stephen Fenwick, Neil Ferguson, Les Hales, Neil Henderson, Brad McElroy, Malcolm

https://doi.org/10.1515/9781501507557-001

Rees, Chris Reid, Graham Roberts, John Steuart and Steve Waller. And many others I have chatted to along the way.

To the current DHL Express teams and their advisors in Germany, Canada, United Kingdom, Hong Kong, Australia and New Zealand who have been enthusiastic supporters and providers of collateral in writing the final chapter, many thanks: Faruk Akosman, Ken Allen, Paul Daley, Charlie Dobbie, Mark Foy, Rick Jackson, Joe Joseph, Mike Lipkin, Dan McGrath, John Pearson, Owen Rees, Susanne Reinecke, Francis Saldanha, Sue Stoneman and Herbert Vongpusanachai.

Thanks to Mark Daniell, John Gattorna and Graham McEwan for their insights, input and advice.

To Pat Lupo, Pete Donnici and Jim Campbell, the three lawyers I would definitely want to hire, and with whom I worked closely during my years with DHL. Thanks Pete for saving DHL in its early battles; thanks Jim for all the good times fighting the postal battles, and for the extensive work on those years which is generously now in the public domain. And thank you Pat for being an inspiring and inspired leader and boss.

I echo Po's acknowledgment to the other DHL Founders: Adrian Dalsey, Larry Hillblom, Robert Lynn, Bill Robinson and Dave Allen.

Lastly, thanks to Jeff Pepper and the team at De Gruyter.

Finally, a dedication to those heroes who are no longer with us: My great mentor Bill Walden, my great mate Bob Parker, and two great characters, Errol Gates and Martin Black.

About the Authors

Po Chung, Co-founder of DHL International, is passionate about the nature and values of superior service required for the success of global centers of commerce, as most developed communities have shifted from manufacturing robotic workers to a people-service economy. His professional life has been dedicated in large part to understanding *how to provide superb service, how to educate others as superior service leaders, and how to design and operate service sector organizations.*

In 1972, Po co-founded DHL International Limited, a Hong Kong based company that, together with DHL Airways Inc. USA, owned and operated the DHL Worldwide Network. The success of DHL is a vivid example of a global people centric network for service.

Currently, as Chairman of Hong Kong Institute of Service Leadership & Management, Po is a champion of the effort to develop service-oriented courses and executive education programs for Hong Kong's eight UGC-funded universities and corporations.

Po is also author of the *Service Masters Editions: The First Ten Yards* (Chinese and English versions), *Service Reborn, The 12 Dimensions of a Service Leader* and *25 Principles of Service Leadership.* Another title under this series, *Pillars of a Service Hub*, is coming soon.

As a thought leader, Po is Officer of the Most Excellent Order of the British Empire (OBE), a board member of many corporates and organizations and in his leisure time, a skilled calligrapher and semi-professional painter, voracious reader and avid student of entrepreneurship, personal and professional development.

Roger Bowie joined DHL as a courier in London in 1976, and went on to management roles in the Middle East, Africa and Southeast Asia.

From 1980 through 1988, as Regional Manager, Africa, Roger led the growth in the DHL Africa Network from 5 countries to 55. In 1988 he was appointed Regional Director for Southeast Asia and Australasia, based in Singapore.

In 1993 he became Worldwide Services Director based in Brussels where he joined Po and four other senior executives on the Global Management Board under CEO Pat Lupo. He resigned and returned to New Zealand in 1995 for family reasons.

Roger's career henceforward has primarily been in healthcare, starting as CEO of Southern Cross Healthcare from 1995 through 2002.

Po and Roger therefore have a unique insight into the history of DHL and what made it successful. Both are featured on today's induction program for new DHL employees.

Contents

Prologue

Company Arrest

Hong Kong, June 16, 1973.

It was Saturday. At that time, all Hong Kong businesses were open on Saturdays and of course, as a service business, so was DHL. That particular morning, as I was leaving home, the phone rang. It was one of our staff, Paul Chan.

"Mr. Chung, the police are here and they want to send some gold. We told them we do not send gold. We explained that we could only send documents and they got very upset. They are seizing our documents and they want to see somebody who is responsible."

The police had, in effect, tried to entrap us since, at the time, moving gold into or out of Hong Kong was illegal unless you had a license. As Paul hadn't fallen for that trick, the police had switched their attention to the documents we were transporting.

Of course, I got to the office on Jaffe Road, Wanchai as quickly as I could. There were a number of policemen there, all big, almost sinister-looking men. I found out later that they were actually from the homicide division! The reason for this was not that they were trying to intimidate us—any more than we would have been intimidated anyway—but because all of the commercial crime people were busy chasing fake five dollar coins that were appearing in Hong Kong. So, the Commercial Crime Bureau had borrowed officers from the murder squad.

Habits in the police force are obviously hard to break, and while the homicide police didn't quite pick me up by the scruff of my neck, they were pretty forceful. Fortunately, the inspector in charge, Mike Prew, was a "white collar" crime man who actually treated me very well.

Meanwhile, Paul had been released and had slipped away to the office's street entrance, where he stopped any couriers from coming in. He sent them straight to the airport so the business continued uninterrupted, except for one bag that the police had seized in the office.

I was then taken to the Commercial Crime Bureau's offices in Fleet House, also in Wanchai. Inspector Prew explained to me that I had nothing to worry about. "We are arresting the company. You are responsible for it, but we don't think that you will have a criminal record."

Of course I was worried! At the time, I had what was known as a Certificate of Identity, not a full passport. With any form of criminal record, it would be very difficult for me to get a visa for any travel outside Hong Kong—not ideal when you're running an international business!

Prew asked me to accompany him to Wanchai Police Station—very close to our offices—for photos and fingerprints. "But," I said, "why take my fingerprints? You are only arresting the company, not me."

"Okay, we will release you on bail of HK$500."

I didn't have $500 on me—it was quite a lot of money to be carrying around in those days—and when I called back to the office, they couldn't raise $500 among the staff either.

https://doi.org/10.1515/9781501507557-002

So Prew said, "Well, you're not going anywhere anyway, so we will let you go. But we will hold on to these documents."

When the police finally opened the bag they had seized, they found 12,000 cancelled checks. This was a matter of some concern to them. They were concerned that the checks might be stolen, but they had failed to understand that these were "dead documents." So, if anyone had stolen them, the checks were worthless anyway.

I left the police offices and considered what to do. The cancelled checks were all drawn on Bank of America accounts, so the bank was my first stop. They sent me to see a lawyer, T.S. Lo, and I told him the whole story.

Lo asked me whether there were any other companies in Hong Kong doing the same type of business as what we were doing. "Of course," I replied. "All the banks and shipping companies are using services like ours." Lo thought for a moment asked, "Can you prove that?" I said, "Give me half a day."

It was actually quite easy to do. I simply went to the airport, bought twenty-five newspapers, and sent them off very quickly to different overseas addresses using twenty-five air freight forwarders that had offices there. This wasn't normal business for them, but they did it for me. I remember Lo being quite impressed with how quickly I had managed to do it, and how extensive the industry had already become. Or so it had appeared.

–Po Chung

In June 1973, when this story took place, DHL had been in business for almost four years and was just starting to get traction, to get noticed. DHL found itself under threat, both in the USA, where it all began, and in Asia, with a few countries open for business. Existential threat. Cease and desist threat. Go away threat. Disappear!

The Hong Kong story is important because this was the first time outside of the U.S. that DHL's right to do business was challenged by authorities. It is also important because this was a territory, a colony of the United Kingdom, governed by the rule of law. Arbitrary judgments did not stand in Hong Kong. The law of precedent prevailed. Lawmakers and enforcement agencies had to be on guard that they didn't act on a whim, a prejudice, or an "arrangement." But "arrangements" in this frontier with China were not uncommon, and intimidation was not uncommon.

It is important also because the people involved in starting this fledgling business felt no guilt about what they were doing. On the contrary, they felt a sense of injustice, of being misunderstood. they had to react; they did not meekly surrender to authority, and they were ingenious in their response.

It is interesting because essentially it was a fishing expedition: smuggling was the assumption, gold was the commodity. And the police were from homicide, not customs—not a more appropriate agency—and they were intimidating. Frustrated in their initial quest, they found another reason to be suspicious. Hong Kong's Postal Law, as in all countries, conferred a monopoly on the national post office for the carriage of letters. The postal monopoly, an ancient concept embedded in statute, had national security as its original motivation. So surely DHL must be in breach of this monopoly? But when it came to trade, to commerce, to the legitimate exchange of monies, to the essence of Hong Kong's raison d'etre, even the authorities paused for thought before enforcing this law.

And, as we shall see in our story, it is a good thing that this took place in Hong Kong, because it is a story which repeats itself time and time again over the ensuing ten years, throughout the world, and in environments more capricious in their application of authority.

This is the story of a little company which emerged with the big idea—elegant in its simplicity, but profound in its impact—of creating a messenger, or courier, service which covered the globe, delivering commercial documents whose value depended on the time it took to get there. Information is perishable, but speed gives life, relevance and value to such information. In those days the dominant medium was the written word, in a document or a check or an image, conceived in one country and consumed in another. It was the link in the chain of international commerce.

The Little Company that Could

But it is more than just a story; this book also offers a framework, a point of reference for today's challenged world, and for those enterprises endeavoring to succeed globally in a world where the idea of globalization has taken a distinctly negative, unfashionable turn. Clear evidence of rising economic disparity in developed countries, with the gap between rich and poor increasing on a global scale, has created global angst, particularly among the Western democracies. And this has occurred despite good progress overall in reducing poverty levels. Loss of faith in establishment elites and their dominance of the political scene has also influenced a rise in populism and a more strident nationalism which also rails against big business.

This is partly a symptom of relative economic decline in the West versus the relative ascendancy of the East; it is partly a leadership crisis as America turns inward, Europe stumbles with its internal market, the UK seeks to exit the EU, and China fails to reassure and convince that its intentions are good. It is partly also because big business has not behaved in ways which earn the trust and respect of global citizenry. The 2008 global financial crisis exposed the moral turpitude of the banking industry, at least the financial trading components. Globally there are worrying signs of consolidation, reduced competition, selfish monopolistic manipulation, and poor governance. Crony capitalism is overtly succeeding in the non-democratic economies and covertly so in the democratic ones. Finally, local citizenry are unhappy about one of the consequences of globalization, the freer flow of people as well as goods. The latter is welcomed, because more can be consumed at home for less; the former is unwelcome, because of perceptions that immigrants take jobs away from locals and other issues.

Conversely, the world has never been smaller, when you combine the influence of cheaper air travel and the internet with its Facebook, Twitter, and other connectivity apps. How to resolve the paradox that globalization has brought cheaper access to goods and services for consumption, yet is blamed for much that is wrong with the world?

One way is for businesses to be better at being global, as they showed they could be in the 80s and 90s. But they were different times, you might say. "How is what happened then, relevant to today?" There was no internet, no online shopping; there were no smartphones. There *was* no globalization in the 80s.

Yes, but there had to be a time of preconditioning for today's world, and *that* was the time: when air travel became faster and cheaper; when shipping became containerized; when sourcing, manufacturing, and distribution became multi-national; when the technologies which created the internet began to be commercialized; when computing became personal; when logistics became a business discipline; and when the platforms for the service economy were laid out.

The service economy is fundamentally different from the manufacturing economy, and the service mindset is fundamentally different from the manufacturing mindset. The former is qualitative, the latter quantitative in nature; the former is measured in intangible and emotional terms, the latter in task and output terms. The former uses automation and mechanization to empower individuals, the latter to replace. The manufacturing mindset is Darwinian in the context of human advancement; the service mindset is Maslovian. More than ever, today's global economy is a service economy; production is just a process between perceiving a customer need and its fulfillment.

This is why DHL, the little company that could, is important and relevant to today's global aspirants, and why this story is also a framework for how to conceive, build and sustain a global business, as well as a platform for leaders to organize their teams to take advantage of the global service economy.

What DHL achieved, in building and maturing its business against all odds, is important for two reasons. First, today's world of speed and connectivity would not work without the support of global logistics and on-the-ground delivery services underpinning business-to-business, business-to-consumer and consumer-to-consumer e-commerce. DHL founded the international air express industry, made it legitimate and built a networked organization to a global scale. In doing so, it changed the way the world did business. Secondly, DHL showed how to harness the soft powers (of finesse rather than force) discussed in detail later in the book and other attributes first brought to our attention by Peters and Waterman in their 1982 book, *In Search of Excellence* and much written about since in the context of nations and competitiveness.

So, this book is both a story and a framework. It is first and foremost a story because it is interesting, we hope entertaining, and analogous to the little engine (company) that could, a story of optimism, determination and hard work. But on looking deeper into the how, as well as the what DHL did which was so interesting, it becomes much more than optimism and hard work. Hence we take you on a journey of philosophical, psychological, as well as entrepreneurial significance as we examine and explain the toolkit of soft powers which differentiated DHL from its competitors, if not its time, and bring those attributes with relevance into a twenty-first century framework. Especially pertinent as the world reviews its relationship with both capitalism and globalization from a populist perspective.

Soft power is the ability to shape the preferences of others through appeal and attraction. A defining feature of soft power is that it is non-coercive.[1] Joseph Nye has written about soft power versus hard power, in the context of politics, political leadership and the behavior of nations.[2] Soft power is the ability to shape the preferences of others through appeal and attraction. We utilize this notion in the context of the behavior of companies, and specifically those doing or aspiring to do business globally or with aspirations to. We might think of soft and hard power as the leveraging of a company's soft and hard assets, and in the former case, the leveraging of soft assets, done well, may emerge as pillars of a company's culture which may be difficult if not impossible to emulate. It is the ultimate in competitive advantage, as everything else a business does will ultimately commoditize, because over time it is easier to copy.

By 1990, DHL had understood, whether intuitively or explicitly, how to leverage soft powers to build a global company from zero. These powers emerged, like biological phenomena, not manufactured or concocted from a test tube. Some of these powers were external, and some environmental. They pre-existed, to be leveraged. Others were, and are today, purely people powers, the DNA of DHL. And, as we shall see in our final chapter, most of these powers have survived and are thought to be so important that they are taught, albeit using slightly

---

1 Wikipedia.
2 Nye Jr, Joseph S. *Soft Power: The Means to Success in World Politics.* New York: Public Affairs, 1994.

different terminology, through DHL's Certified International Manager (CIM) and Specialist (CIS) programs. They are described throughout our story in both generic and DHL specific contexts and are part of the culture that is unique to this organization

Our hypothesis is that the soft powers that matter, in the case of DHL and for many other organizations, can be distilled into twelve groups:

1. The power of time, place and environment: being in tune with the times or just ahead—but not too far ahead—and being at the same time, in the right place. Some might call this the power of luck, others may counter that it is not luck, but being available. Linked to time and place, the choice of location is important in the context of environmental support for global activity. As we will discuss, the rule of law, maritime versus continental mindsets, and language feature here as important to being successful globally.

2. The power of universal products and having "first mover" advantage: having global appeal. Being valued everywhere. Making changes which benefit all. DHL did a lot of this with a simple product. And DHL did it first.

3. The power of customer focus and alignment: DHL went wherever its customers wanted. It made outrageous commitments to customers and then delivered. Over time, it learned the art of segmentation, first intuitively, and then systematically, understanding that the internal supply chain of service delivery demanded a different response based on customer need.

4. The power of vision and mission: the mission statement is important here, but this is also about the balance of missionary and mercenary in how a business behaves. What type of capitalism is in play? Where does corporate citizenry come in?

5. The power of culture and values: the way we do things around here, our unique DNA. The soft power which differentiates you from the competition. Trust is also critical.

6. The power of positive psychology: people wanting to come to work, and leaders who fail if they don't.

7. The power of the three Cs: character, competence and care, plus, collaboration, and a host of other Cs.

8. The power of network and organized best practice: how to organize globally, how to simultaneously think and act locally and globally. DHL was a global network before it had a head office. The network was *the* asset. DHL was also organized to capture and promote best practice.

9. The power of optimized flow: echoing a recent hypothesis which claims to discover a new natural law of physics, the evolution of DHL's network and

operating systems is all about continuously improving the efficiency of moving goods around the globe. A modern day, clearly visible example of evolution in action, it is comparable to what we might see in nature as common design principles, such as the way a river flows or a tree grows.[3]

10. The power of partnership: partnering in business is both a skill set and a mindset. Sometimes it is mandatory, sometimes it is strategic, sometimes it is pragmatic. Whatever the circumstance, partnering only works if both parties work hard at it, like a marriage.

11. The power of the brand: DHL's brand emerged after ten years of activity, and merged seamlessly with a people-driven culture. The people as the brand, as well as the brand itself.

12. The power of leadership: leadership from the founders, leadership from the front and from behind. More bottom-up than top-down. The leader as Renaissance man or woman. Being generous as a leader.

This is not a recipe; it is more a set of ingredients. DHL didn't have a grand plan; a lot was intuitive or picked up along the way. We hope you will get insight as you plan or refine your own global strategy, and we also hope to entertain you with a good story.

---

3 Bejan, Adrian, and Zane, J. Peder. *Design in Nature*. New York: Doubleday, 2012.

DHL Chronology (1969–1990)

Incorporation: DHL Corp	1969
DHL Philippines	1971
Incorporation: DHL International Hong Kong (DHLI)	1972
DHL Japan, Singapore, Australia	1972
CAB cease and desist battle	1972–6
DHL New Zealand, Fiji, Indonesia, Malaysia, Thailand	1973
Hong Kong postal fight	1973–5
Incorporation: Federal Express, DHL London	1974
DHL Amsterdam, Paris, Tehran	1975
Pan Am fight begins	1975
DHL Bahrain, Saudi Arabia and Mexico	1976
DHL Canada, Korea, Germany, Norway, U.A.E, Kuwait	1977
DHL word processor (with Arabic)	1978
DHL Nigeria, Caribbean, Brazil, Colombia, Venezuela, Greece, Ireland, Belgium, Sweden 360 service centers, 85,000 customers, Bill Walden appointed CEO	1979
DHL South Africa, Kenya, Argentina, Denmark, Spain, Lebanon, Oman DHL Regions created; DHL Chile, Uruguay, Bangladesh, India, Sri Lanka, Austria, Cote D'Ivoire, Zimbabwe, six other Caribbean countries	1980
MRI established in London. Postal monopoly suspended in UK	1981
DHL Global Conference in Athens, 17 new countries added, Service to 30 new countries	1982
Service to Eastern Europe, 24 new countries and US domestic	1983
Service to 18 new countries	1984
Brussels hub opens, plus seven new countries	1985
Pat Lupo as Global CEO, DHL China joint venture, plus service to 11 new countries	1986
Service to 7 new countries	1987
Global Headquarters opens in Brussels, service to 3 new countries	1988
DHL celebrates 20 years; Service to 175 countries, 19,000 employees	1989
Japan Airlines, Lufthansa, Nissho Iwai acquire first tranche of DHLI	1990

https://doi.org/10.1515/9781501507557-003

Chapter 1
Born Global

This is a book which tells a story: the story about the little company that could; the little company that thought that doing business globally could be enabled by faster connectivity, in a physical, pre-internet world. The little company that pioneered global express delivery services and overcame regulatory barriers which governed postal, customs and logistics activities.

The little company which recognized the time sensitivity of commercial correspondence between and within companies doing business internationally. The little company which built a global network predicated on speed, reliability, security for the physical movement of those intrinsically valuable business assets.

The Little Company Which was Seen as Illegal in Every Country

In 1969, Larry Hillblom and two older colleagues, Adrian Dalsey and Robert Lynn, formed DHL (using their surname initials), a courier service providing door to door delivery of time-sensitive documents between San Francisco and Honolulu. It was a time of intense change and opportunity. It was a few short months after Neil Armstrong stepped on the moon, with immeasurable social impact and a challenge to the world to acknowledge and embrace the mind-boggling technology involved. On the other side of the spectrum, however, the prospect of technological change had come just far enough to inspire this unfunded start-up, far more quietly, to change the world and the way it does business.

Dalsey, Hillblom and Lynn (D, H, and L). 25th Anniversary party, 1994

https://doi.org/10.1515/9781501507557-004

The initial capital invested was a few thousand dollars. The rest was put on credit cards. It was too much for Robert, and he left, leaving behind the "L." Adrian Dalsey, the "D," supported early international expansion before falling out with Larry over the prospect of an early sale of the business. Larry, the "H," effectively steered the fledgling business through its entrepreneurial phase to challenge the status quo of international shipping, to become a global upstart. He then withdrew to pursue other activities, while maintaining a close watch and influence from a distance. Thus, began the business career of the man who, according to a recent biographer,[1] "made globalization possible."

This book is not about Larry, or the other founders, but the brief quote above is an entirely appropriate starting point for our discussion. Indeed this book is about the hundreds if not thousands of people who, together, created the extraordinary culture of DHL, and who collaborated to achieve Larry Hillblom's legacy, to effectively change the world of business. We will not specifically name those people, but we will reference Larry and other founders such as Dave Allen, Bill Robinson and Po Chung, not only as key influencers of the DHL philosophy and culture, but also as evidence that DHL was never an American company, but was instead a nascent global from birth. We will also profile the key leaders, Bill Walden in the 80s, followed by Pat Lupo in the late 80s and 90s, as well as the key legal counsel who collectively over the years saved DHL from premature extinction.

Fundamentally, this book is not about individuals: it is more about the ideas, the philosophies, the culture and the context of the times which underpinned a period of relentless innovation that established a new way of doing business that has evolved a bit, but survives today. It is more about the drive, the heroics, and the happy accidents which supported a great idea and turned an entrepreneurial effort into a crusade from which emerged one of the earliest truly global companies of the modern era. And it is about the barriers which were ultimately overcome as change, and fear of change, combined with regulation and history to protect the status quo. From start-up, to upstart, to the most international company in the world.

In this context, we leave the people's stories, of which there are thousands, (and which deserve dedicated if not autobiographical publication) to other efforts. Instead we concentrate on their collective activities and achievements in building a global business which paved the way for the globalization phenomenon which characterized the last two decades of the 20th century.

---

1 Scurlock, James D. *King Larry*. New York: Scribner, 2012.

Any story of this nature inevitably relies on a chronology, and we can segment DHL's chronology broadly into decades. The 70s comprised the start-up, entrepreneurial phase, with an almost single-minded focus on building up the global network as DHL's major asset.

The 80s was a decade of continued growth, but also maturity, as systems and processes were broadened and institutionalized under a more classic corporate structure. But investment in consolidation necessarily had to sit alongside continued rapid growth, which created the classic phase two (in start-up terms) pressures of capital and cash flow. In this decade, brand emerged as a significant intangible asset, and early management philosophies were polished into an emerging corporate culture. Diversification was also a hallmark of this decade, as customers increasingly asked for an extension of the core service into parcels of all sizes and content. Moving from a single homogenous product line, carrying documents of no commercial value, to offering a small parcel express service for dutiable items was not as simple as it reads. There was considerable variability in approaches to levying customs duties on items with an extrinsic commercial value. Further, concern about the impact of technology and emerging electronic data transmission as a substitute for physical document carriage also drove investments into new technologies designed to keep DHL ahead of the game. Increased competition and huge market growth also forced the rapid accumulation of physical assets, hence the pressure on cash. Few companies survive this critical phase of development.

The 90s saw a transformation of a relatively simple, courier service product suite into the complexity of a nascent integrator; the move to offer the same express solution for dutiable goods as well as documents. This was the time that the term *logistics* entered the DHL lexicon, and the fact that DHL actually achieved this is nothing short of astounding. External investors certainly helped, but ultimately the completion of DHL's journey from courier to a full-service delivery provider did not occur until the new millennium, when Deutsche Post paid the ultimate compliment to the founders' vision by acquiring DHL outright.

Our story will not go that far; instead we will concentrate on the first two decades, following (but not slavishly), the chronology, preferring instead to examine four themes which emerge from a retrospective look at a business in its journey from start-up to upstart. Along the way, we will examine the factors that enabled this "company that could" to endure. And, at the end, we will see how a company closing in on fifty years has been able to maintain the same basic values and work ethic that made it survive in those difficult start-up years.

What are those themes?

The road DHL has taken throughout its history has been dictated to a large extent by these four themes:

The business environment: What was it like in those times? How was business done? How did people think when they built a business? What were the challenges and how did DHL overcome them?

The market: How did DHL's services change the market? What drove customers to demand DHL services? How did customers and competitors help shape market growth and DHL's response? How did a brand emerge?

The regulatory environment: Why was it like it was? How did DHL approach seemingly-interminable barriers to make it possible to continue to do business, for itself and for its emulators?

Philosophy and culture: Finally, but not least, what thoughts, ideas, backgrounds and experience coalesced into a functioning system for going global and building a sustainable leadership cadre and culture?

This is the story of DHL as a disruptive, innovative force, perhaps unlike any other force until the internet of things allowed the Amazons, the Googles, the Facebooks and arguably the Ubers and Airbnbs to once again challenge the existing views of building and operating a global enterprise.

Chapter 2
The 70s

DHL was incorporated as the 60s came to an end, a decade which saw the post-war baby boomers challenge, if not cast off, the straightjacket cultures which characterized their parents' life views as they recovered from the trauma of World War II.

The 70s, however, was a vastly different decade, one which challenged the hedonism and optimism of the 60s in more ways than one.

In the USA, the country was at war with itself as it faced a dubious outcome in Vietnam, and as conservative middle America reacted against the hippie culture to elect and re-elect Richard Nixon, whose dark moods mirrored the uncertainty of the times.

In Europe, economic turmoil lead to an expansion of the European Union from six to nine countries, a move that was both a political and economic turning inward. The United Kingdom, in particular, experienced a decade of relative decline, both in terms of global influence as well as a stagnant economy beset by industrial unrest. The Soviet Union was becoming more recalcitrant in the face of US political turmoil, and China reached out, tentatively, but prematurely, as the Cultural Revolution lingered on under the Gang of Four.

In 1972, Palestinian terrorists struck at the Munich Olympics, and England and Ireland saw an increasingly active Irish Republican Army (IRA). Global insecurity was further impacted by perhaps the defining event of the 70s, the oil embargo of 1973, which created economic turmoil in the developed world. The impact of a huge surge in the price of oil meant stagflation, high unemployment as well as inflation, effectively ending the postwar, Bretton Woods era of fixed exchange rates and capital controls.

As the decade progressed, America was consumed by the Watergate affair, proof that politics are often dirty, opportunistic, and that the highly moral and idealistic posturing of political leaders jostling for the nation's highest offices are sometimes just masks in a dirty game of charade. "The president is a crook," heard not for the first time, and certainly not the last, took on a devastating new meaning when actual evidence about Richard Nixon emerged. The president resigned rather than be impeached. America arguably lost both confidence and innocence during this time, recovering momentarily in the world view with the success with the Camp David Accords between Israel and Egypt, before being challenged again by the Iranian Revolution. The hostage crisis, which lasted over a year and humiliated Carter, resulted in another Cold War warrior president to

https://doi.org/10.1515/9781501507557-005

emerge in the form of Ronald Reagan. Meanwhile, the Russian bear continued to growl, as détente, which had progressed in the early 70s, fizzled, and the Cold War, once again, intensified.

Socially, the younger generation moved from extroversion to introspection, as music trends showed with the rise of progressive rock, a misnomer in the context of the prevailing mood shifting from optimism to angst, often aided by mind-altering chemicals. Then it was back to extroversion in the face of disillusionment with the political system.

In short, this was not an environment conducive to globalization!

On the contrary, the prevailing regulatory frameworks which existed throughout the western world were protectionist in nature.

Postal laws which entrenched monopolistic rights to national postal systems had their origins in the Middle Ages, when insecure monarchs created a framework for monitoring communications between citizens and across borders.

Postwar insecurities and prevailing mind sets of "never again" produced customs and trade frameworks designed to promote and then protect local industry from international competition. Customs processes were consequently deeply bureaucratic, also in line with governments' self-appointed role to be job creators, as importing and clearing goods became an Orwellian nightmare game of "pass the parcel."

However, global trade was still a significant component of the world economy, no matter how constrained by regulation, driven by technology and in no small way a consequence of the emergence of the oil cartel. Planes became bigger, with room for more passengers and more freight. Ships became faster, and containerization revolutionized port handling processes and reduced transit times between ports, which meant that supporting processes such as sending shipping manifests also needed to speed up. Telecommunications improved such that regular long-distance phone calls became both possible and within economic reason. The telex machine turned the telegram into an everyday office tool. Oil exploration boomed, as the search for more and cheaper fuel drove oil companies to more obscure parts of the globe. Banking grew as a consequence of increased inter-country and intercontinental financial transactions, and important deregulation started in the USA, affecting air transport and opening up protected skies to more open competition.

And so, in certain quarters, this time of economic and political upheaval, concurrent creativity and freedom of expression also generated or produced entrepreneurial individuals whose minds turned to commerce, with or without the support of mind-changing drugs, and whose frames of reference went beyond conventional borders.

The obvious examples are the two Steves, Wozniak and Jobs, who founded Apple, Bill Gates and Microsoft, Richard Branson and Virgin. Here were determined individuals of contrasting styles and personalities, be it shy or swashbuckling, but involved in high profile technological and travel sectors which were "sexy" if not in name, then in public perception.

Transportation of goods, was, in contrast, decidedly unsexy and under the radar. Logistics (which as a commercial term did not actually emerge until the 80s) focused on getting finished goods distributed to end customers. There was no thought at this time of integrating the sourcing of raw materials with production and distribution as we will see in the 80s and 90s.[1] Logistics in this sense was still very much a military maneuver. In transportation, there were a number of entrepreneurs, including John Emery of Emery Airfreight (to become Emery Worldwide), Sir Peter Abeles of TNT and Gordon Barton of IPEC, but the two standouts were Larry Hillblom (and colleagues) and Fred Smith (Federal Express). They were two very different characters who focused on the small items which the freight forwarders found uneconomic, and built large networks which relied on economies of scale to generate margin. In short, Larry and DHL chose the international market as a playing field; Fred chose to concentrate on the USA (still, after twenty years, a larger market in terms of volume). Fred was an Air Force guy, who brought the discipline and structure of military logistics to package delivery. Larry in comparison was a free spirit, who spoke the (at the time) heresy that governments should be promoting not restricting/controlling commercial activity. Both DHL and Federal Express were, in effect, born in the 70s, and have become global colossuses, along with UPS, a much older company, built essentially on industrial engineering principles.

Engineering, military logistics and imagination fueled the new thinking about courier or express services which emerged from the dark early years of the 70s to support and indeed promote international trade and the emergence of the global corporation, which in turn fostered a new wave of globalization.

Globalization as an in-vogue term didn't arise until later, but it wasn't an original concept.

One can go back to the great migrations, of which there is still much to learn, as homo sapiens spread throughout the globe. More recently, we reflect on the age of sail and then steam, which allowed the great maritime nation of the United Kingdom to win the colonial empire-building race against more continental powers such as France, Germany, the Netherlands, Spain and Portugal. Global trade

---

1 Gattorna, John. Dynamic Supply Chains: *How to design, build and manage people-centric networks*, 3rd Ed. United Kingdom: Pearson Education Limited, 2015.

flourished in that era, and indeed became a mantra justifying all sorts of injustices to be imposed upon innocent peoples, whether they be subjects or targets. That era of globalization arguably brought accelerated prosperity to much of the world, but within a European paradigm of colonization and hegemony, and which ultimately ended in global conflict.

The globalization of which we shall speak arises from the aftermath of World War II which unleashed a new era of nation building and distributed global political power and influence. That, along with the "never again" mind set in the developed world, fostered the emergence of protectionist "space" to allow each new nation to build their own security through self-sufficiency. Ultimately inefficient, ultimately constraining, this system was ultimately to be challenged by a new wave of globalization driven by the multi-national, or "nation-less" corporation of which DHL was an early, if not the first, example.

Finally, this was also the decade where the service economy starts to emerge as a fundamentally different beast from the manufacturing economy, with its qualitative versus quantitative mindset and its measurement based on intangible and emotional terms, rather than in tasks and outputs. The service economy is based on moments in time when two people interact in performing a task which provides mutual benefit. A service business succeeds when those moments can be repeated time and time again, and nuanced according to the situation. The equivalent manufacturing paradigm asks for consistency and homogeneity, not spontaneity and individuality. Building a global business based on service rather than manufacturing principles requires new ways of thinking and organizing.

Chapter 3
The Start-up Years

In the early 70s, to send urgent documents overseas there was a choice (short of taking it there yourself!) between using the postal service or sending via airfreight. Postal services were not designed nor mandated to deal with urgency, especially urgency which could be defined by how much more than postage fees the sender was prepared to pay. On the contrary, postal services were governed more by principles of universal access and affordability: the same service for the same price, no matter whether you lived in the country or city.

Similarly, airfreight, a mode which was made possible by advances in airplane technology arising from World War II, focused on consolidating packages into large units of freight, to maximize efficiency and space utilization of what was a relatively expensive commodity, the belly space of aircraft. Small packages either had to wait until they could fit in with large ones, or run the risk of being mishandled as a low priority (in handling terms) by the agents involved. Pricing for small packages was subject to a minimum charge, typically 45 kilos.

Then the phenomena of regulatory protection, mentioned in Chapter 2, would kick in. Complex processes for import and export, characterized mainly in terms of paperwork, as well as multiple handling agencies, created very complicated and laborious supply chains which, like the postal services, were not built for speed.

To send via airfreight, first, a freight forwarder had to be engaged to pick up the package and take it to the airport. Often, shippers of small packages would be told to bring it to the airport themselves! Then it had to pass through an export process, using a customs broker (someone licensed to process on behalf of customs). Then through customs, then to the airline. Someone else, such as an airport handling agent, or a general sales agent, might do this. This process played out in reverse at the other end, a service or supply chain of so-called specialists handling each process, each with their own unique ways of doing business: selling, invoicing, accounting, etc.

The problem would become more acute if shipping involved more than one sector, or multiple destinations. This could take days, if not weeks, and would be very complicated. No firms would handle the end-to-end service of sending something from A to B to C. Instead, it would be cut up into lots of different service and transport segments.

Small wonder that the big freight forwarders didn't want to deal with the small stuff; small wonder that when they did, the service was low priority and

https://doi.org/10.1515/9781501507557-006

subject to lots of mishandling. And it was particularly galling if in fact the package was comprised of just paper and didn't require export clearance, or indeed was considered duty-free at point of entry. That stuff was for the post office, anyway. Post offices had special handling, priority shipping, and customs-free clearance, because they were a trusted institution, and knew how to handle letters for final delivery (customers brought the letters to them for dispatch, so collection wasn't an issue).

The problems were further exacerbated by the way airlines (and behind them government regulators) gave priority to what could fly. Passengers and their baggage came first, then perishables, then post, and finally general freight. The lonely individual package of documents didn't stand much chance of being given royal, reliable, rapid service.

And, finally, no-one worked at night. Even if flights came in late at night or early in the morning, the ground handling and customs processes staff typically worked daytime hours.

What about Matson shipping (and shipping companies in general) who took advantage of faster ships to provide a better service, only to stumble because shipping manifests (detailing the goods being shipped) failed to arrive in advance of the ship? In deference to production efficiencies, shipping documents, required for import or clearance at destination, were more often than not prepared after the goods had left. This hadn't mattered in the old days, when ships were slow, and the post generally got there. But in the early 70s, even between San Francisco and Honolulu (no customs!), delays in getting the shipping manifests through meant that ships were stacked up at port entry, and were being charged for taking up space while waiting. Time, in this context, was truly money.

And the banks, whose letters of credit enabled the financing of import and export across national borders? Delays in clearance processes due to payments not being made also caused grief. Specifically, Bank of America had a different problem in Hong Kong, where hordes of American servicemen serving in Vietnam took their leave and cashed their U.S. paychecks, drawn on U.S. banks. The longer it took to get those checks cleared at origin, the less the bank made on the transaction, or, conversely, the more discount the poor servicemen had to accept for immediate value.

And, increasingly toward the end of the decade, what about the oil companies such as BP, and related construction companies such as Brown & Root? Anxious to break open the oil cartel and increase production, this typically meant going to remote new geographies or already difficult locations in which to do business. How were they going to get their business mail, their construction drawings and other documents through in a reasonable time frame, if at all?

Larry Hillblom saw a solution for the shipping companies. He had already put himself through law school by being a courier for a company based in Los Angeles, which offered a service to and from San Francisco. He had already spent those years flying himself up and down at night, sleeping in airports and studying by day. His imagination easily extended that experience to doing the same thing across the world.

Thus, DHL started by Larry flying himself back and forth between San Francisco and Honolulu, every night, unless someone else wanted a free trip and some time off in Hawaii. There was no shortage of those people in those days! Listening to the shipping and banking guys, understanding their problems and offering a solution was the early hallmark of DHL's success.

Soon the customers wanted to go into Asia, and the business expanded, with Adrian Dalsey (the D) still involved as super salesman, picking up Po Chung in Hong Kong as a DHL International partner.

Another pioneer was Bill Robinson, an early franchise partner of Larry's in the U.S. when the fledgling corporation expanded as a franchise model before being obliged to consolidate into a single entity under the CAB (Civil Aeronautics Board) ruling (to be discussed in Chapter 7). Bill took an early lead along with Adrian in exploring international locations, such as the Middle East, and identifying local partners. Bill was the quiet intellectual type that kept everyone on track, writing piercing but humorous commentaries on ideas which he felt had not been thought through, and he was an early advocate of corporate culture. The humor in his criticisms taught the early founders how to laugh at each other. That is an enduring legacy. For a while he was president of DHL Corporation, until the early 1980s. Then he slipped behind the scenes and played a backseat role, principally advising Larry on DHL corporation issues while Larry concentrated on international service or expansion and his 1980s activities in Micronesia. Bill returned to play a critical role in the U.S. in the 90s and 2000s.

It was Bill who found Dave Allen driving a taxi in Sydney. Dave and Po became the two international founders of DHL. These individuals collectively defined the key characteristics of the DHL culture: the relentless drive of Hillblom, the salesmanship of Dalsey, the evangelism of Dave Allen as he led the expansion into Europe and beyond, and the more philosophical nature of Po as he thought about the DHL people.

DHL grew exponentially when word got around to customers who required a service which was not being offered by the post office or airfreight forwarders. Bank of America was so convinced of the value of DHL's unique service that it paid in advance to provide working capital to finance expansion into Southeast Asia.

The early DHL years were characterized by the typical challenges of a start-up, and also driven by the personality of the founder—relentless, demanding, working harder than anyone else, spendthrift, building loyalty without compassion, but through the force of the idea and commitment to it. Using personal credit cards, shuffling cash flow through credit card arbitrage, and infected by the founder's enthusiasm, the early leaders all had, or adopted, the habits of the entrepreneur. Keeping costs down, creating shortcuts, pushing the boundaries, leading by example, never ever giving up until the idea then became all-powerful, as reflected by customer demand, and took on the evangelistic nature of a movement, to ultimately morph into a global business.

Easy to say; easy to write, but far from easy to do!

Chapter 4
The Start-up Years: Business Innovation

Door to Door, Desk to Desk

Postal services were not satisfying the level of urgency experienced by businesses in getting important documents to their destination on time. The late arrival of important documents created delays which cost businesses money. Airfreight forwarding as an alternative was cumbersome, with a fragmented system involving multiple players whose independence served to increase cost and slow things down. Countries built their regulatory frameworks to protect local businesses and enhance national security, not encourage international firms to enter their markets and compete. Improving service and lowering costs for everyone was not a priority.

In order to ship packages or goods through the airfreight forwarding system, a number of players were traditionally involved. Airfreight forwarders, import and export agents, customs brokers, airline cargo or freight agents or general sales agents (GSAs) were required as well as the airlines themselves. Also, customs and other government security agencies, such as food and agricultural safety departments, were part of the chain. This supply chain duplicated itself at origin (export) and destination (import) and repeated itself multiple times through a package's journey if multiple sectors were involved.

The impact of all of these players involved in handling, processing, moving and inspecting goods in transit was twofold: extra cost (as each player charged for their services) and, more significantly, extra time. Each time a new player played their part in the supply chain, time was lost.

DHL's great innovation was to see things in their totality, door to door, desk to desk, and provide an end to end service without any middlemen being involved. Even if DHL had agents in certain countries (i.e. companies performing an in-country service because DHL was not allowed or chose not to set up its own local company), these agents all participated seamlessly in the DHL supply chain such that the customers perceived it as one DHL service, not several services joined up by disparate parties. Speed was one feature, but consistency, reliability, and control were also features which customers quickly came to value. Only one phone call if things went wrong, and, as we discuss below, only one invoice for the entire service.

https://doi.org/10.1515/9781501507557-007

Just Like Taking It There Yourself

DHL was a pioneer in the concept of "messenger" across regional, national and then international borders, by flying couriers on board. DHL couriers were normal passengers with their own tickets, who carried customer deliveries as passenger baggage instead. This cut tremendous amounts of time down both before the aircraft departed, and after it arrived. Cut-off times for passenger check-in baggage was nowhere near as long as the four hours required for cargo. In those less security-conscious days, at most airports, checking in bags one hour before flight time would suffice. If, as DHL couriers and their colleagues almost always did, one established good relationships and familiarity with the airline, one could be last onboard, which added precious minutes to activities on the ground.

After reaching the destination country, baggage could be cleared in as little as half an hour, assuming that none of the baggage contained dutiable items. Assuming also that the same degree of relationship and familiarity existed with people involved in the arrivals process.

This modus operandi also avoided the fickle nature of prioritization to interfere at the last moment when aircraft load-balancing occurred. Ultimately the pilot has a veto on how much cargo is carried, dependent on passenger load and other factors, and freight with a lesser priority was "offloaded" (for this, read not loaded at all). The passengers and their baggage were always a number one priority. It also helped with another bottleneck that could occur if goods had to change planes at an intermediate airport (transit point). Goods in transit on the cargo side were subject to a similar fragmentation of service that occurred pre-export, and post-import. Lots of processes, each one taking time! Conversely, passenger bags checked through had the same priority as a passenger. The time saved on arrival processes through passenger baggage as opposed to freight allowed for faster connections if a package was to leave the care of one courier to join another on a connecting flight. Often a courier could be met at a transit stop, drop off and collect new material, and then continue on the same flight. If it was a once-daily flight schedule, this process would save twenty-four to forty-eight hours over existing methods.

This might seem obvious from today's retrospective view, but it was very new in the 70s! And of course, the parallel picture being painted here is not just of innovative business practice, but also the idea that time saved at each point in the journey was money saved or cost avoided.

It was a simple idea, but of course an expensive one when you compared the cost of a ticket and the rates charged per kilo for excess baggage as opposed the cost of airfreight. Not so expensive though, as taking it there yourself!

Still Expensive, However, for a Start-Up ...

Obviously, DHL couldn't afford to fly couriers on every plane, particularly as expansion provided exponential growth in the number of routes (pairings of cities) which were to be served. To clarify, three cities served comprise three routes, but four means six different routes to be flown. The combinations quickly multiply.

Another important factor here is the different approach in the U.S. to charging for accompanied baggage. Within the U.S., and to the first outbound destination, airlines charged accompanied baggage on a piece rate basis (a fixed price per piece of baggage, regardless of weight). There was no restriction on the number of pieces or strict adherence to weight per item (as long as it could be handled) that we see today. Internationally, however the convention was to limit the total baggage allowance per passenger (say twenty or thirty kilos) and charge an exorbitant rate for excess baggage (a proportion of the first class airfare, per kilo was a typical formula). On the one hand, this convention was an effective deterrent to passengers exceeding the limit; on the other hand, it was prohibitive to the idea of a courier carrying hundreds of kilos, unless a compromise rate was negotiated. Over time, the economic advantages of flying couriers from the U.S. was eroded as the piece rate practice disappeared; conversely airlines also began to see commercial advantage in offering discounts for excess baggage in exchange for the guaranteed sale of a seat on every flight. But flying couriers was still an expensive approach.

So, airfreight as a method was still used to keep costs down, and allow for volumes to grow to the point where a courier on board became more viable. It might seem counter-intuitive that using airfreight, a mode of transport which we have hitherto vilified because of its complexity and aversion to speed, was still central to the business plan. But it is not so counter-intuitive when you consider four things:

First, the courier was not just the person on the plane, it was also the courier who went to the customer's office to make the collection, as well as the courier at the destination making the delivery. In Larry's case, as he started the business, this was literally true, as he himself flew every night, making pickups and deliveries during daylight hours, until business grew to the point where others could be recruited to do the flying.

However, if DHL didn't or couldn't afford to use the courier-on-board method of getting things moved by air, and instead used airfreight, they were still managing the entire service, unlike airfreight forwarding, where many different parties could be involved.

Second, it was possible, to build similar relationships on the cargo side of the airport as was achieved in the baggage halls, particularly while one was relatively small (small enough to be cute, or novel, as opposed to being a nuisance). "Under the radar," is another applicable term, which allowed many routes in the early days to be effectively serviced by airfreight, because the overall door to door transit time was still much, much faster than other means.

Third, at the end of the day, the method itself was not the issue; it was whatever optimized the flow that mattered.

And finally, the courier-on-board approach was always a means to an end. The objective was always to achieve the same sense of priority and speed of processing from the passenger terminal to the air cargo side of the airport.

... and Increasingly Complex

Constrained by lack of cash, and faced with increasing demand, this hybrid system grew and with growth, came the exponential complexity referred to above. How to manage the ever-increasing number of route combinations economically, and maintain the astounding level and consistency of service which kept customers asking for more? As Ernest Rutherford said, in relation to his work on splitting of the atom, "we haven't got the money, so we'll have to think."[1]

A process of progressive consolidation evolved, to reduce complexity and increase both accuracy and speed of sorting at transfer points. Transfer points were airports which were intermediate points on a package's journey, where a process of deconsolidation, sorting and reconsolidation took place. Often transfer points were also major origin or destination cities, and so packages picked up from, or destined for, that city were also put into the mix at a transfer point.

Early experience at what quickly became the busiest transit airport, Hong Kong, translated into the simple but elegant innovation of using colors and coding, and reversible transfer bags, to facilitate rapid consolidation and reduced chance of error.

The first consolidation took place at the customer's dispatch office, where lots of small envelopes of varying sizes were grouped together and put into a nylon pouch. The pouches were unique, in that they were color-coded, representing the origin, and labeled with the three-letter IATA (International Air Transportation Agency) airport code for the destination. The pouches had the customer's name and were used for customers who had regular (daily to weekly) dispatches to the same destination, and vice-versa. So Citibank's pouch, for example, between London (LHR) and New York (JFK) was pink for New York, and labelled

---

1 As recalled by R.V. Jones, *Bulletin of the Institute of Physics* (1962), 13, No 4, 102.

LHR, in red, white and blue for London. The pouches promoted loyalty, increased frequency, and accuracy. They also made great beach bags, and were often seen on beaches on weekends.

Citibank London's pink pouch for New York was then grouped with all other packages for New York on that day (some in similar pouches, others in their original packaging) and put in to a larger duffel-type "transfer" bag, again colored pink, but this time reversible. On the inside the color was for the origin city, in this case London. When the bag arrived in New York and had cleared customs, it was pulled inside out, then all the individual packages were guaranteed to be emptied out, and the bag was ready to be filled with London-bound material. The transfer bags therefore always traveled the same route, and were easily spotted if they ended up in the wrong place on the sorting floor, or occasionally misrouted. And to put "occasionally" into context, early testimony to the U.S. Civil Aeronautics Board claimed such systems and control minimized mistakes to seven per million individual consignments.

Finally, all transfer bags were further consolidated into larger, green canvas bags which became the units of shipping for airfreight, or to accompany on-board couriers. Green bags typically weighed twenty to thirty kilos, so that they could be carried or moved by one person, and also so that they could qualify as passenger baggage.

At transfer points, green bags were opened, their contents disgorged, sorted, and regrouped according to where the contents were next destined. Local transfer bags were further emptied and sorted for delivery routes.

All this sounds terribly organized and structured, but the reality was that transfer points were often airport halls, airport carparks or loading bays to freight terminals, and the process was untidy and frenzied. Time was always short, hence the genius of the color and airport codes, and reversibility. It was easy to see from a distance if a pouch or transfer bag was in the wrong place. It was also intriguing for other passengers or passers-by to see this flurry of activity and color occurring in open spaces!

So, Try and Keep It Simple

Keeping things simple in an era where there was little technological support and zero automation was an ongoing challenge. In those early days there was no internet, and fax machines were not yet commercially available. There was the electric typewriter, the telex machine, and the telephone, still very expensive for international calls. There were no conveyor belts, no mechanized sorting systems, just manual, paper-based processes. And finally, there were no computers to process billing and tracking.

The pouch, transfer and green bag system was one way to simplify. One other innovative way was in the pricing structure.

Postal services were priced by weight, typically grams and kilos (or ounces and pounds), and zoned into broad geographical regions dependent on distance and/or popularity.

Airfreight services were priced similarly, by kilogram, with minimum weight thresholds (to keep out those pesky small parcels) and zoned, but in much more granular fashion than postal regions. But there were also handling charges at origin and destination charged by the individual businesses who comprised the complex supply chain described earlier. There were lots of hidden charges, if you took the entire journey into account, and tried to understand the total cost of shipping, some of which was charged to the sender, some of which might be charged to the receiver.

The postal approach was obviously simpler, but didn't differentiate between frequent and not so frequent users.

DHL's super salesman founder "D" came up with a simple hybrid between the two prevailing options: a "handling" fee and a rate per kilo (pound), regardless of destination. The handling fee was either per shipment, or per month, which created a generous incentive or frequency discount. Just two options, to keep it simple, as there was no computer to process complex billing algorithms. The frequency discount (monthly handling fee) typically kicked in if a customer used the service more than once a week. Add to this the fact that it was an all-inclusive price, door to door, no hidden costs and as fast as taking it there yourself, and you had a compelling selling proposition.

One can safely assume that having a salesman determine the pricing mechanism meant that scant regard was paid to actual costs, but that didn't matter in those days when speed, convenience and ease of administration were the driving factors. Outside of the USA the per pound rate became a 1/2kg (500 grams) minimum, as pricing crossed into the metric zone, and distance was recognized by zoning. The essential simplicity of that first pricing mechanism lasted a long time, confusing competitors and cost accountants alike for years and creating competitive advantage along the way.

So Simple, Almost Too Good to Be True

DHL charged one price, door to door. This price initially appeared to be high, because customers did not fully appreciate the total cost of shipping when so many players charged for their piece of the action (clipped the ticket), and when often costs were shared between shipper and receiver (for example, shipper pays export, receiver pays import). So, the initial reaction was to use DHL only for extremely urgent documents—described as time-sensitive, in that their value diminished with time. The early customers, as we have seen, had a compelling reason to compare DHL charges to their opportunity costs such as avoiding demurrage charges incurred by ships lining up to enter ports. And once salespeople started to compare and contrast the total costs as well as the hidden costs (time wasted), then conversely, DHL's charges were seen to be very reasonable.

But initially, there were many customers who either didn't believe the promise, couldn't conceive of the value, or both.

And the promise was speed, consistently, reliably, along with convenience (door to door) and simplicity (one all-inclusive charge). Getting something delivered overnight between San Francisco and Honolulu, London and New York, and two days (taking time zones into account) between London and Sydney, or San Francisco and Hong Kong, was unbelievable. Next day from London into Saudi Arabia was off the planet!

Proof was Needed, and So Proof was Provided

Each shipment (envelopes, pouches, packages which made up a single consignment) had a multi-ply airwaybill (AWB) with a unique numerical identifier, which often had to be completed manually at the time of pick-up. Ironically, the need for an AWB came from the first regulatory battle which Larry encountered, when he faced a Hobson's choice of whether to be considered an airline or an airfreight forwarder by the USA authorities. The airline option was prohibitively expensive, the airfreight forwarder option involved a lot of paperwork, and neither category actually described the activity undertaken. Nonetheless, part of the requirement to be registered as an airfreight forwarder was to use an AWB according to international law and convention. So the AWB became a multi-purpose document, serving as an invoice, a collection receipt, a manifest, a delivery receipt, and a proof of delivery. Because proof of delivery (POD) was a key selling point, it became standard operating procedure to return that slip of paper to origin. This was an enormous logistical endeavor in and of itself, manually intensive and time consuming, as couriers had to be trained to religiously keep the delivery slip copy. Further, a summary manifest was also drawn up listing each shipment consigned to a transfer bag, which was checked off when the bag was emptied at destination. Then each courier drew up their own manifest, or delivery schedule, which was often also signed by the receiving customer. Sometimes these manifests were also returned to act as a back-up if the (smaller) POD didn't show.

The return of the proof of delivery served as a key selling point, as well as a means of dealing with complaints. Especially the all-too-frequent example of a package being delivered and mishandled or misplaced within the customer's office at destination.

Other forms of providing proof were of a promotional nature to help make the sale for example, the sending of newspapers so that expatriate business men could keep up with the news at home, or the sending of last night's rugby game by video to be shown to a bunch of rugby enthusiast businessmen the next night in some remote location.

Proof of delivery naturally enough became a customer expectation, which in the context of the complexity in sending thousands of small items economically and speedily through a matrix of geographies, often exceeded the capability of an essentially manual, paper-based process. This expectation, as we shall see later, drove more than anything the subsequent investment in technology and electronic data transfer which characterized the 80s.

But back in the 70s, at the very least it ensured that the transfer bags were regularly rotated, even if returned empty except for a bunch of little yellow POD slips.

With the Airlines as Friends (Albeit Fair-Weather)

As discussed in the chapter about regulatory battles, DHL didn't have a lot of friends in those early days. Relationships with the airlines, the essential component of this burgeoning international supply chain, waxed and waned over the years. But relying on commercial carriers was a fundamental strategy.

In contrast, Fred Smith launched his business, Federal Express, in 1974 with the explicit and core strategy of owning everything, and this specifically meant investment in aircraft. Of course, his initial focus was U.S. domestic only, with the service proposition of everything being deliverable overnight, for instance, between any two major cities within the USA. In this context, commercial carriers could not provide the service, as passengers preferred to travel during the daytime. Federal Express' hub-and-spoke system, whereby everything was flown into a centralized geographical hub in Memphis, sorted and then flown out again, required absolute control of the take-off and landing schedules of the aircraft.

In economic terms, this meant that the aircraft needed to be almost always full, or there would be a step-cost investment phase in unused capacity while volumes on any given route built up, because aircraft don't come in incremental shapes and sizes. Once a small aircraft was full a bigger aircraft is needed, and therefore the company is investing ahead of the curve until volumes catch up. This issue of having to invest in unused capacity created a further challenge if trade or commercial flows between any two countries or cities were unequal. An aircraft might go out full, but come back half empty. This situation gave rise to the "back-haul" problem, whereby other freight needed to be found to make up any route imbalances.

Take this scenario international, and the imbalance problem on key long-haul sectors was entrenched in decades of trade imbalances which still exist today.

DHL's use of commercial carriers was both pragmatic and strategic. Pragmatic because flying its own aircraft was not only cost prohibitive, it also required flying and landing rights which were jealously guarded by national carriers. Also, commercial carriers on long-haul sectors often did fly at night, and so having your own capacity didn't confer any advantage in terms of speed of transit. Finally, it meant that costs would rise incrementally in line with volumes, and not step up suddenly when a new or larger aircraft was required.

It was strategic because first, it enabled national airlines to view DHL as a customer and not a threat (this came later), and second, it enabled DHL to maintain flexibility in its cost base, and avoid the step cost and back-haul trap. This state of events was to be tested in later decades, as FedEx exported its model globally, as airlines themselves saw competitive opportunity in replicating DHL's service, and as growth in volume and service expectation outstripped commercial capacity and capability to provide an optimal level of service to DHL customers.

DHL's business took off. Customers loved the simplicity, and marveled at the speed. It was not only novel, it was intriguing, and to be talked about. Word of mouth became a key driver of growth, and DHL's innovations began to change the way the world did business.

Chapter 5
Innovation and Its Broader Impact on Business Dynamics

The 70s saw rapid and exponential growth, a relentless pursuit of network expansion driven by customer demand. By the end of the 70s, DHL's network had expanded to cover 360 cities in forty-five countries. Each time a new city opened up, the possibilities for sales expanded several-fold as the routes expanded exponentially. Every delivery to a new recipient was an opportunity for a new sales pitch. Specifically, DHL's entry into the Middle East at a time when oil exploration was rampant, and the ability to move documents quickly into the most remote and difficult locations served as a catalyst for opening up, for example, secondary commercial centers in Europe. Expansion occurred at a helter-skelter pace. What on earth was going on?

DHL's early innovations were driven by a proactive vision, fine-tuned by an intrinsic and intuitive ability to listen to and respond to customer issues. Those innovations, largely without technology, built the process flows which characterize the activity of any express or courier service to this very day. But it was more than just process.

The Infectious Nature of Speed

In today's world, we are overwhelmed with information, its ubiquitous nature, and the speed with which it gets disseminated. Disruptive technologies are challenging our traditional, and not so traditional habits and ways of doing things, and proliferate at a pace which is hard to keep up with. The 70s, on the other hand, were relatively sleepy and slothful, until DHL challenged the business world, and specifically the worlds of transport and post, with the notion that things could be moved faster and the consequent time saved had considerable value. It wasn't just the opportunity costs which were being discovered and eliminated, the entire experience of getting things moving faster and faster became infectious within the DHL tribe. Stretching the airlines to accept baggage or freight at the last possible minute, or racing the rush hour traffic in central London to get something delivered before the office closed became a daily competitive challenge, against the elements, against the established ways of doings things. The value proposition in the eyes of the customer, as those eyes were opened by the seemingly pretentious little start-up racing around in

https://doi.org/10.1515/9781501507557-008

old cars with disheveled, sweaty drivers arriving at the front desk, was all about the value of time.

The concept of time-based value became entrenched as a fundamental principle of international commerce. Speeding things up, in short, created economic value everywhere in the supply chain, and value was monetized in so many ways—reduced interest costs, faster access to funds, greater certainty, less risk, more competitive terms of trade, more time to complete tender documents. All these opportunities were realizable with the arrival of a service which recognized the time-sensitivity of content in commercial terms. Just as the value of news diminishes with time, so too can important commercial information. Just like the fresh produce which held a high priority in accessing airline cargo space, because over time it perished; so too was information and content perishable.

Size Doesn't Matter, Content Does

And, often, just like precious stones, the smaller the medium for the content, the more valuable it was. But small items were handled by the post offices, characteristically large government-owned monopolies with huge workforces who were more often than not unionized and by their very nature, slow. They were certainly not customer-friendly or responsive to the needs of international commerce.

And freight forwarders, even those with extensive international networks, didn't like the small stuff. The process of international freight forwarding implicitly, if not explicitly, discriminated against the small parcel, through pricing (high minimum weight pricing thresholds) and the multiple handling nature of the service process. By innovating and intervening throughout a small package's journey, DHL was able to progressively aggregate and disaggregate hundreds of small items into mini-consolidations, which made handling easier, more secure and of course faster. In other words, small items on their own are more at risk of being misplaced or mishandled. Putting small items together into a bigger bag or container reduced this risk. It also meant that individual shipments didn't always travel by the most direct route. Hubs, or transfer points, were used, to ensure larger volumes per route were maintained. Most often, this system of consolidation, break down, and transfer did not compromise door-to-door speed, because transfers and consolidations occurred at night.

Keeping It Dense

This ability to consolidate was also evident in the nature of the market segment which DHL targeted. This was the Business to Business segment or B2B, as it is more commonly known in today's parlance. Individual customers and home deliveries were rare in those early days. Conversely, because businesses tended to be clustered within central business districts, or special industrial zones, delivery density was easier to achieve. One courier could spend minutes in a tall building or industrial zone delivering to different customers, which might take hours if the customers were at unique addresses in suburban settings. At a more micro level, the provision of pouches to large customers also encouraged consolidation and a single point of pick up or delivery within a customer's office, typically the mailroom.

But Keeping It Simple

As already discussed, pricing was kept simple and encouraged frequency of use. Remember this was a world without commercial computing power, so discounting had to be simple in order to maintain efficiency of billing and invoicing. Delivery density also meant that couriers would often call on a customer because it didn't take much time, just to see if anything was in the pouch. What might well have been not so urgent that it could wait until tomorrow, often went today!

And Everyone Sells

As we will further explore in the next chapter, one of the key features of DHL's concept of door to door delivery was the management of the "last mile." Just as in any long distance race, the last mile often became the stumbling block for airfreight forwarders in that so many things could go wrong. Many freight forwarders did not want to do collections or deliveries; post offices promoted P.O. boxes. DHL's founding partners all participated in the courier experience; they all did pick-ups and deliveries in their early days. They quickly learned the value in managing and controlling the last mile, even the last yard, of the service, and this was instilled in all the couriers who succeeded them. Not only were relationships built with the customers deep inside their organizations, for example with secretaries and mailroom managers, but also every delivery became an opportunity to make a sale, and so, in early DHL culture, everyone was a sales person.

Service Is Not Servitude

The importance of first and last yard of any value chain has been eloquently described in Po Chung's own book on entrepreneurship, "The First Ten Yards."[1] In early DHL days everyone was a courier, everyone was a salesman, and everyone was taught to think strategically. But something more fundamental was going on here. Service and service jobs had hitherto been seen or perceived as menial, something to be done, but not aspired to. DHL couriers were different. They were young, enthusiastic, smiling, friendly and articulate. They knew what had happened to ensure the delivery was achieved so quickly, they knew how the emerging system worked. Being a courier in DHL was not being at the bottom of the pyramid, it was being an integral part of the service chain. Being recognized by the DHL leaders as so important, not just for the pick-up and delivery function, but also for the intelligence gathering and salesmanship which accrued from the relationships being built with customers, heralded the emergence of a service culture and mindset, which in many countries had been hitherto absent or alien. Messages such as "I saw this or that competitor in our customer's office today," or "company Z wants us to go to country Y," mixed with ideas about small service improvements or other ways to improve the customer experience, all bubbled up for attention in this most egalitarian of worlds. The idea of service as a passion, not driven by extrinsic financial gain (tips) but intrinsic self-worth as a reward in itself, is emphasized.

There is a deeper change happening here. Maslow's hierarchy of needs, which is universal in its applicability, deals with the progressive journey of personal development through the stages of physiological needs, safety, love/belonging, self-esteem through to self-actualization. The emergence of the service economy, and the service mindset is significant here.

The maritime/Anglosphere culture and predisposition, elaborated on in later chapters, arguably provides a platform from which a corporate environment can nurture and support an employee's journey through the Maslow stages. The emergence of a service culture within DHL has Maslovian consequences in terms of the early leadership and its ability to spread the service culture across the globe. The personal commitment to service through war, natural disaster and upheaval became a universal attribute of the DHL culture. It can be argued that DHL's early development was in fact a vehicle for individuals to move up the hierarchy toward self-actualization.

---

1 Chung, Po and Ip, Saimond. *The First Ten Yards: The 5 Dynamics of Entrepreneurship*. Singapore: Cengage Learning Asia, 2009.

Creating a Time-Based Value Proposition

By offering a door-to-door, all-inclusive service with one price, DHL removed the complexity for customers who no longer trusted the postal service and were frustrated with dealing with all the disparate parts of the airfreight supply chain. DHL achieved this by doing it themselves, or managing those bits it didn't physically own. DHL also sped things up. Customers were simply amazed to get their packages days or sometimes weeks faster than traditional methods.

This was what later became known as disintermediation—removing the middlemen from the supply chain. By providing a door-to-door service, DHL bypassed all the players, or simply embraced them as part of the DHL system that oversaw the package's journey. From the customer's perspective, they only had to deal with one company, pay one price, and make one phone call if things went awry.

Disintermediation has in later decades become a clarion call for most innovative businesses seeking to make a difference, improve service and lower costs for customers. DHL was pioneering this concept before the word was invented.

Challenging Traditional Work Habits

Traditional methods of work were challenged, particularly methods used by customs authorities. Customs processes in almost every country were traditionally bureaucratic, complex and, because speed was anathema to control, subject to fraudulent intervention (small bribes or "kickbacks"). To put this in context, remember that customs processes were built to inhibit, rather than encourage imports. By their very nature as government agencies, they were also invariably overstaffed and those staff were poorly paid. Opportunities were everywhere, particularly in the developing world, for "clipping the ticket": small favors in exchange for getting things done.

By creating a sense of urgency, by being persistent, persuasive and familiar, DHL made things go faster, and the faster things moved, the less time there was to intervene and demand a kickback. Yes, occasionally there were favors dispensed but invariably these were in kind, rather than cash. DHL's philosophical view was that first, DHL customers wanted service to this or that country, and therefore one had to be flexible to get things done; but also, unrelenting in the pursuit of eliminating corrupt practice over time, if not refusing to take part from day one.

And in the Spirit of Partnership

Many entrepreneurial start-ups fail to make good partners. They often fail to mold successful partnerships because of their entrepreneurial myopia, an inability to see beyond their own core competency or to trust others with their expertise. DHL's early ability to forge partnerships with the airlines might have been a necessity in terms of economics, but it also served DHL well as it continued to expand at a pace which placed great demands on available cash. From a cultural perspective, what was at play here was a natural (i.e. in their nature) tendency of DHL people to reflect the American/Anglosphere trait of "winning friends and influencing people," in contrast with the tendency, that one might argue exists in more authoritarian worlds, to buy friends and manipulate people.

The sorts of operational partnerships which DHL entered into in the early years involved countries which were either too small to warrant a direct invest-ment, or where regulations either required international service companies to have a local partner, or reserved the service sector to local enterprises only.

In the former circumstances, the relationship was typically one of principal to agent, with DHL the principal. Compared to these markets, there were bigger priorities in terms of bigger countries with more global customers wanting service to them. So, all DHL required was a good service inbound. In the bigger markets, however, DHL treated local partners as principals, not agents, and accorded them the full respect and attention they deserved as partners/members of the burgeon-ing DHL network.

Partners came to conferences, and were treated royally whenever they trav-eled. And they were well-incentivized; typically, focused on building outbound traffic. In turn, these partners were enraptured by being part of something which was going global, and growing rapidly. They eagerly embraced the DHL pro-cesses and procedures, and supported DHL when local regulators came threaten-ing. They became full members of the DHL family.

The above dynamics highlight the impact of DHL's process revolution as it built its worldwide courier service. After years of watching DHL people succeed in getting things done faster, companies and indeed countries began to see the economic value of speeding up commerce.

Speed truly became infectious ...

Chapter 6
Cultural Dynamics: What was Going on Here?

Against All Odds

In the 70s, DHL created a new business model which disrupted existing channels for moving urgent documents across the world. As a result, customers had a new set of expectations: fast, secure, reliable, consistent—all of these expectations bundled up into a single all-inclusive price.

It wasn't easy building this business; there were practical as well as regulatory issues to resolve. Often the customers would be aware and support efforts to overcome logistical and legal barriers. But once a certain level of scale was achieved, many customers also expected that DHL ought to have taken care of any problems before they came up, in the general context of compliance which they were already accustomed to in their own fields of endeavor.

But, as we shall discuss in the following chapter, DHL was deemed to be illegal in virtually every country it operated in. It was either in breach of the postal monopolies, or suspected of smuggling illegal contraband through customs (why else would they want to do things so fast?). Or not paying tax, or contravening all sorts of other regulatory frameworks into which the fledgling courier company didn't quite seem to fit.

Ahead of its Time

The business process innovation which enabled rapid growth across international borders was impressive. Many of the principles involved were precursors to business models which emerged time and time again as businesses became global. The KISS principle (keep it simple, stupid), the disintermediation principle, the customer comes first principle, the total supply chain principle were all examples of fundamental practice which later became norms. But in the 70s these hadn't been seen before, let alone labelled.

It was also the People

So what was the recipe, or the secret ingredient which allowed DHL to innovate and overcome seemingly insurmountable barriers at the same time?

https://doi.org/10.1515/9781501507557-009

The Maori in New Zealand, the indigenous ethnicity whose culture underpins what it means to be a Kiwi, have a famous saying: "He aha te mea nui? He tangata, he tangata, he tangata" which translates: "What is the most important thing? The people, the people, the people."

DHL people were different, they came from all over the world, and it took a special kind of person with special characteristics to challenge the status quo in pursuit of an idea. An idea which supported businesses to function all over that world, yet was being challenged on several fronts. The DHL people, the way they went about their business, and the way they thought about their business, provided the diverse cultural base from which emerged, over 20 odd years, a unique corporate culture. The intangible "the way we do things around here" which, in a world where any new innovation is copied and eventually commoditized, provides the ultimate competitive edge.

The 70s saw the first stages of the emergence of a corporate culture which set the benchmark for how global corporations should operate.

We said at the beginning that this book is not about the individuals, but it is important to reference the founders, those whose early influence on DHL endured in the emerging corporate culture.

First, we had Larry, whose character combined the entrepreneurial drive of a visionary and confrontational style of the litigious lawyer he was trained to be. Larry was always right, and would often start a conversation in aggressive lawyer mode, immediately putting his interlocutor on the defensive. But he did do the hard yards, and worked harder than anyone else in getting something to work; then he expected others to pick it up and make it sustainable. Larry was more like Steve Jobs, or, more accurately, Steve Jobs was more like Larry, relentless, demanding, building the loyalty of the acolyte, respected and feared in the same emotion. But the "H" was right more often than not and always ahead of his time. DHL people couldn't help but be impressed with his vision, and more congenial characters picked this up and turned it into a mission.

Adrian Dalsey, on the other hand, couldn't have been more opposite. Older, greyer, opportunistic, Adrian was the consummate salesman from whom you would, contrary to popular myth, buy a used car. While the "D" didn't last long in DHL, he did set the pace in terms of the silver tongue of the salesman, selling something almost as unbelievable as snake oil, but far more real in the execution. DHL didn't have many people in "sales" throughout the 70s; it was all about operations, getting things done. So, there was none of the typical gap which invariably occurs when salesmen, eager to achieve the sale, over-promise, and operations struggle to deliver. On the contrary, operations people eagerly sold the service as they went; there was none of the stigma about being a salesman which

Robert Kiyosaki tells of in his book "Rich Dad, Poor Dad."[1] Because, in early DHL, everyone was in sales. In fact, one of Dalsey's sayings was: *"If you're not picking up or selling, you are not working."*

Bill Robinson was the iconoclastic intellectual, sitting behind the scenes, damning with faint praise, and teaching the others to laugh at themselves. An essential quality considering the challenges they all faced, and one which endures to this day.

The two international founders, Po Chung and Dave Allen, were both entrepreneurs with the rare qualities of empathy and congeniality, not typically found in the classic profile of the relentless entrepreneur.

Dave Allen

Dave, an Englishman, was "discovered" by Bill Robinson, who was on a visit to Sydney to set up the business there. Dave was on an overseas working holiday, playing rugby and driving a taxi. Nothing pretentious here! Dave was quickly seduced, and joined DHL by setting up the Sydney office, and then returning to London to set up the operation there. This was the time (70s and 80s) of the great

---

1 Robert Kiyosaki and Sharon Lecther, *Rich Dad Poor Dad*, Warner Business Books, 2000.

"OE" or overseas experience, which saw thousands of young baby-boomer Australians and New Zealanders set off, with a few dollars in their pockets, for overseas destinations without any preconceived idea, but to get as far away from home as possible. Dave was recruited for this unproven, literally fly by night, crazy courier service. He went to work, tapping fellow colonials, rugby players from the London rugby clubs which the Aussies and Kiwis frequented, some of whom Dave knew from his days in Sydney. Augmented by a smattering of South Africans and Rhodesians, this group of young men and women easily and enthusiastically embraced the "adventure" of making DHL work, not just in London, but first in Europe, then the Middle East, then Africa, and also forming the second wave of management in Southeast Asia. Dave was not only a born salesman, but he had the natural leadership style and bonhomie which made working all hours, being ready to jump on a plane and move to another country at a moment's notice, taking risks with the regulatory authorities, in short, qualities which made building DHL a fun thing to do. Working hard, playing hard, and then working hard again, was the credo. The folks in DHL USA looked incredulously at this maverick bunch of irreverent people, and referred to them as "Dave's cowboys."

Earlier, Larry and Adrian had found Po Chung in Hong Kong. Po was no less of an entrepreneur than Dave, and certainly anglophone in outlook (or "maritime" as we will come back to), but he was also Asian, and more philosophical and thoughtful in demeanor. In particular he thought about what was important to sustain DHL as it rushed to expand a very American service concept into different countries and cultures. In Po's own words:

> I was also playing the role of the philosopher, working to set up systems. There was important work to be done in adapting, evolving, or even coming up with new practices entirely in the process of moving the company from a local one to a global one. Nothing could be taken for granted when we were expanding into a multi-cultural, cross-border situation– what worked in the States didn't necessarily work overseas. We had to rethink a lot of things, like our business practices, cultural assumptions, the ways in which we dealt with our clients, and so on.

While Dave's cowboys ranged from Europe to the Middle East, combining the colonial traits of egalitarian respect for all people and fearless disrespect for the rules, things in Asia had to be approached differently, because virtually everyone was local, there were few, if any, expatriates. Particularly in North Asia (known as the Far East), people both respected and feared authority, and so the prospect of DHL's very existence being challenged as it was in Hong Kong by the postal authorities did not go down well with the local couriers, some of whom were too frightened to continue to come to work. Po dealt with their issues by resorting to the innate family values which bound social structures as well as business in

Asia. This focus on the "softer" values which nowadays are known to underpin corporate culture, was critical to DHL's ability to attract and retain key personnel in challenging times, and key components to what we shall later describe as the DHL difference and framework for going global.

An Emerging Company Culture

Taking a west coast American idea and translating it into a global network; providing consistent, fast service which was respected by customers all over the world required stamina, courage and persistence.

The DHL founders each brought attributes to the kind of corporate culture which is necessary to operate across the world. In the 70s, that culture was just beginning to emerge: a blend of the fearless, aggressive, visionary entrepreneur; the fun-loving, optimistic, never say no style of the expatriate Englishman and his colonial followers, themselves equally fearless; and the Asian family values which united the growing cadre of Chinese, Korean and Japanese citizens undertaking a risky venture in their home countries. In those times DHL USA, DHL Asia, and DHL Europe and the Middle East were still more different than alike, but a common sense of purpose and ethic were starting to unite them into something unique–an emerging global enterprise.

The Nature of the Business Helped

Blending the best characteristics of each of the founders was one thing; but the business itself also played a big part. For a start, it was, in contrast to the cultures of the countries where it took place, pretty homogenous from day one. Everyone did pick-ups and deliveries. Everyone had color-coded pouches. Everyone had similar types of customers trying to solve similar problems. Everyone treated their customers as kings. For the most part, everyone was young. And when they got together they had things in common. And each of them could share experiences with the others, many of which became legendary, but which invariably involved people going out of their way to serve the customer. Or being confronted with impossible situations which required fast thinking and decision making on the spot. The key thing, of course, was that each DHL employee partook in a service need which was conceived in one country and fulfilled in another. They worked together, even if they couldn't see each other. Especially because they worked together at a distance, they learned to trust each other, and this quality, this blind trust, more than anything started to shape a more homogenous culture, and one which can be better described in the context of the 80s.

But it Wasn't Just the Business

In the frenzied years of the late 70s, when growth accelerated, especially as a result of entering the Middle East, DHL people felt more part of a movement than a global corporation. The level of trust, the level of independence, the freedom to learn, make mistakes and learn faster, created a sense of personal ownership of a business which oddly at that stage, had no head office. Besides, it was a great product, a great service, of course it must be legitimate, and of course it was just the right thing to do. As a consequence, it was on the one hand an almost evangelical fervor which drove DHL people to go the extra mile. On the other hand, as DHL couriers created relationships and friendships deep inside the hierarchies of their customers, and as DHL people grew up together all across the world, it wasn't just business, it was fun, and it was personal.

Chapter 7
Barely Legal—Early Regulatory Battles

"Congratulations, you've started a business which is illegal in every country."[1]

–Lawyer from Brazil

It was perhaps not by accident that DHL was founded by a lawyer, albeit one who never actually practiced professionally. That didn't matter; there were plenty of university colleagues, be they fellow students or former lecturers, who could help with the little things which came up when the world was being challenged and changed.

Over the years, many people tried to translate the meaning of DHL. A few early wags suggested Dewey, Huey and Louie. Competitors larked "Documents Hopelessly Lost," but if you were to count up the legal bills which were incurred over the years defending DHL's very right to exist, you might postulate: "Don't Hire Lawyers."

Joking aside, the fledgling global entity had plenty of battles to fight over the years. First, it was deemed by postal authorities to be in breach of the postal monopoly in almost every country. Or it was surely an agent for the CIA. Such was the aura of mystery which enveloped this motley crew who insisted on speed, speed and more speed in moving goods across borders, clogging up the airport baggage carousels with their suspicious looking green bags, and then creating momentary mayhem as the bags were opened and smaller bags flew everywhere, only to disappear again into more green bags. There must be something hugely illegal going on?

Peter Donnici (Pete) was a law professor at the University of San Francisco and also practiced in private. Larry was a former student who contacted him sometime in 1972 with the story outlined below, that the United States District Court had just recently ruled against DHL in a lawsuit brought by Loomis Courier. When Pete agreed to take the case (initially pro-bono), Pat Lupo was his law clerk. Once that case was done, and Pat had graduated as a lawyer, Pete suggested that Larry take Pat on as general counsel for DHL Corporation (USA). Thus began a long business relationship as well as friendship between the three lawyers as they battled to win DHL's right to exist.

---

1 Lawyer from Brazil, as recalled by Jim Campbell, DHL counsel. (He went on to add "that's just brilliant. No wonder no-one else has thought of this before.")

https://doi.org/10.1515/9781501507557-010

As the struggle extended into what became a global struggle against postal authorities, Jim Campbell Jr. came into the picture. In 1975, Jim was a staff attorney for the United States Senate Subcommittee on Administrative Practice and Procedure, working under Senator Ted Kennedy, when he met Larry and was also employed as DHL legal counsel. Jim focused on regulatory affairs, principally postal regulations, and this began a journey across the world supporting DHL in the various arenas of battle. Jim was also instrumental in setting up the early industry associations in Europe.

And finally, Geoff Cruikshanks, was plucked from the ranks of DHL's UK law firm in 1981 to become DHL International's in-house legal counsel, a post which he effectively held for more than thirty years, including as his last role, counsel for the entire DHL Deutsche Post Group.

These three individuals, along with Pat Lupo, the future CEO, collectively supported DHL through its existential battles and all of the story outlined in this chapter and Chapter 15 owes a great debt to their efforts.

First, What Kind of Business Is This?

Ironically, the first major battle took place within the USA, prompted by a competitor complaint, suggesting DHL was acting like a commercial carrier but without a license. In its third year of operation, DHL was given the afore-mentioned "cease and desist" order, because it did not have proper certification from the United States Civil Aeronautics Board (CAB). Moreover, the CAB had refused to issue such authorization.

DHL was trying to expand internationally, and the CAB was the authority who oversaw airlines, the licenses for airfreight forwarders, and so on. Back then, things were very heavily regulated. Every year, the CAB would charge airlines a fee of around $150,000 per year to file tariffs. This wasn't a problem at all for the airlines, but for a start-up like DHL it was prohibitive. It was one of the barriers to entry in place that protected the airlines from being challenged by start-ups. Definitely hire a lawyer.

The irony of the "cease and desist" order was that the CAB were treating DHL as if it were an airline. But DHL had no aircraft, leased or owned, no pilots, no passengers. What was happening is that DHL's major competitor, Loomis, was using its connections to get rid of an upstart competitor, and one which had recently refused to countenance an offer to sell to them outright. Loomis was counting on the "cease and desist" order to be followed by a summary judgement. But the further irony was that Loomis was doing just as DHL was doing, and also without an operating airline license. Larry's new legal team appealed and obtained a temporary stay of the order pending the appeal. The appeal lasted nearly two years. They also filed an antitrust/unfair competition lawsuit against Loomis, and a lawsuit against the CAB for wrongfully denying DHL an operating authority. In time, the appeal was won; Loomis settled the antitrust suit with cash, and the CAB settled by granting DHL operating authority, but with conditions. First, DHL could operate not as an airline, but as an airfreight forwarder. DHL was forced into the lesser of two regulatory evils, namely the airfreight forwarder category, when in fact what DHL was doing was not covered by either of the existing frameworks. Nonetheless, registration as an airfreight forwarder required that all shipments travel under an airwaybill (AWB) which then became the multi-purpose document described earlier, and significantly, the proof of delivery. Tariffs also had to be filed and approved, and, second, a further condition was the need to separate DHL's international businesses from the U.S .business. DHL was required to consolidate its small U.S.network of local franchises into a single entity, and divest the non-U.S. domiciled businesses, which at this stage were comprised of a handful of Asian countries. Thus DHL International was born, as an arm's length (in legal terms) business partner of the U.S.based DHL Corporation. This first regulatory battle continued over several years, until the CAB itself came under scrutiny for its arguably corrupt practices in overseeing regulation, which an increasingly trade- oriented political system was seeing as a barrier to effective competition for U.S. firms. Incidentally, Federal Express was also constrained by restrictive CAB rules which meant they were able to fly small aircraft only, which quickly became a capacity issue as their domestic volumes grew.

Ah, You Mean You Carry Mail?

But this early skirmish was nothing compared to what was to come. In 1970, the U.S. postal service was effectively corporatized. The newly formed U.S. Postal Service flexed its new regulatory muscle by extending the definition of letter in its monopoly provisions and awarding itself sole discretion and oversight of any exceptions. Battle lines were drawn for a decade-long legal and political struggle, interspersed with interventional harassment of both operators and users of courier or express services.

And in June 1973, when DHL International was just over a year old, the Hong Kong Police seized one day's outbound shipments, ostensibly in search of contraband. When nothing was found, the charge ultimately became one of breaching the postal monopoly by carrying letters.

Postal monopolies were created in the fifteenth and sixteenth centuries as a state security mechanism, to control communications, essentially to allow for censorship and examination of what content was being disseminated by messenger service or other means. Governments built up the postal monopolies and over time packaged them as a "public good" service. But the original purpose was security-related.

In other words, the postal monopoly was a concept that was some 400 years old. The key part of the postal monopoly regulation which tripped DHL up, and which everyone focused on, was the inalienable right of the national post office to carry letters.

So, what constituted a letter? The postal monopolies were written more or less to define a letter as personal correspondence, and the initial arguments raged around this issue. However, in those early days, arguments that the law was essentially anachronistic and not designed for the needs of modern day business fell on deaf ears, and at the end of the day, the power of the law was on the side of the incumbent.

In Hong Kong law, the definition was so broad as to include any message by any medium, not just paper, as long as it was personal in nature; so, arguably, a restaurant menu, or indeed at the extreme, a tombstone, could be defined as a letter. There were also exceptions, such as a messenger carrying letters on behalf of an employer. Well, then, one judge allowed, an enterprising messenger could well incorporate himself into a limited company, such as DHL had done.

Then there was the issue of size. Monopoly definitions usually characterized a letter by being approximately 100 grams in weight. But DHL was defining and charging for shipments based on a minimum weight of 500 grams (½ kilo). Surely the definition of letter was not intended to extend to heavier items? And when the charges were ten, twenty, sometimes fifty times that charged by the post office?

The fights surged and abated in a variety of jurisdictions as attention was brought to local postal authorities of this growing courier service activity. Various legal arguments succeeded in winning a reprieve, such as in Hong Kong, but the concern about DHL's activity (and those of its smaller imitators) reached fever pitch in the deliberations of the Universal Postal Union. The UPU held five yearly congresses which were largely intended to settle the issues of how volume imbalances were to be settled among the member countries, a payment mechanism known as *Terminal Dues*. In one such congress in the 70s, the corridor talk was about this "cancer" which was DHL. Like an invading disease, DHL cherry-picked the profitable business routes and the delivery-dense central business districts, leaving the poor postal service to pick up the hard to reach rural areas under its legislated universal access mandate. The UPU urged members to excise this cancer before it was too late.

DHL's customers didn't care about postal monopolies. They wanted service to more and more countries as soon as possible. So DHL people ignored the threat of prosecution, and indeed jail time, and carried on until there was an initiative from a given postal authority to respond to. Reckless? No, more practical, because the power of the law was such that any attempt to seek permission was likely to fail, or tie DHL up in extensive and expensive litigation, as the incumbent monopolist exerted its deep pockets in defence of an outdated concept. A "Catch-22" situation, indeed.

And the responses came in a variety of forms and processes. In Paris, in 1976, the French Postal Authorities started writing to DHL customers explaining the illegality of what DHL was doing. Then they arranged for airport customs to seize one particular day's inbound bags (about twenty, say 400kg). French lawyers had been engaged to ensure DHL was appropriately registered to do business in France, an issue which was typically overlooked for too long in many countries by Dave's cowboys, too busy getting the deliveries done! The lawyers took one look at the letters and advised the Australian manager (who had no work permit) to close down and leave. But no, that advice was ignored, and happily the bags were released the next day by a new shift of customs officers who chose to ignore the earlier instructions from the post. This was a not uncommon phenomenon: either the authorities themselves were unsure of their ground and acted via another agency, or those other agencies themselves took an independent view of the matter. Or it was just too much hassle!

The Italians in Milan acted in the very first weeks of DHL's new operations there, and insisted that everything coming in have postage stamps affixed, to pay for the inferred domestic postage. The enterprising young Londoner in charge of Milan, on his first assignment abroad, dealt with that inconvenience by showing the stamps to customs, but not actually sticking them on. They were consequently reused more than once. The Italian Postal Authorities never knew whether they were getting their replacement revenue or not.

The Hong Kong fight was initially won on a technicality, but it was only a reprieve, as the postal authorities came back a year or so later with new legislation. This was designed to close any loopholes, such as the one which allowed the interpretation of messenger to include a special purpose company acting as messengers for customer "employers." This posed an existential threat to Po Chung and his "family" of couriers. The response, and one which repeated itself in various battlefields over the coming years, was to create a coalition of customers, supported by DHL managers from all over the world, to convey to the local authorities that DHL's service was an economic necessity for them to operate, and good, if not essential, for the local economy. This ability to organize a "posse" of managers from all corners of the globe proved to be an effective tactic time and time again. And winning a legal battle against the incumbent monopoly in Hong Kong proved to be both unique and an important precedent. Thank goodness it was liberal, maritime, rule of law Hong Kong where this battle took place!

South Korea in the 1970s was a country still effectively under military rule, albeit with an elected strongman president who was determined to modernize the country and develop an export economy. The political environment was anti-communist and security conscious. Only in 1976 were licenses granted for the freight forwarding industry, and one such forwarder was approached by DHL to act as agent. He started tentatively in early 1977, mindful of legal advice that warned of potential trouble with the postal monopoly and national security agencies tasked with censorship of all forms of international communication. Sure enough, after about six months of modest activity, he was ordered to cease and desist. Once again, the DHL family, or posse, rallied to the cause. Several of the early DHL leaders, including the founders Larry, Dave and Po, spent five months on and off in Seoul, helping to build support through approaches to customers, foreign embassies, export trade associations and newspapers. Some of the nation's key infrastructure projects were being delayed by slow delivery of essential documents, a situation exacerbated by the suspension of DHL's service. Mr. Bae, DHL's intrepid local agent, decided to take the case to the highest levels, and in due course the issue of courier services became top of the agenda at a regular meeting of the Export Promotion Board, chaired by the president of the nation Park Chung-hee. As a consequence, new legislation was introduced, among other things, giving the president the authority to suspend the postal monopoly. DHL service to South Korea resumed on January 1, 1978.

In the U.S., the protracted battle waxed and waned, with progress toward the end of the decade on establishing important principles for determining how exceptions or dispensations from the monopoly regime could be considered. Namely, the definition of time sensitive, being determined by a combination of the service level achieved (hours rather than days) and the premium price over postage that customers were prepared to pay. These principles were important precedents in establishing grounds elsewhere in the world for achieving compromise, short of outright deregulation.

At the end of the decade, after ten years in business, DHL managers and legal advisors had built up considerable expertise in dealing with efforts by the postal authorities to inhibit, if not prohibit activity. And the battles continued throughout the next decade, with recycling of the same old arguments. Ultimately, however, the legal idiosyncrasies only served to delay and incur costs in fighting what was essentially an issue of economics, as opposed to the principles and definitions of monopoly. The economic reality, that time had value, ultimately prevailed. Information was perishable, and courier services were an essential component of the supply chains which were growing rapidly as globalization took root.

But DHL also had to be pragmatic and flexible in maintaining its very right to exist without disrupting service to customers, who by now depended on a consistent reliable performance, and who had their own battles to fight in their respective regulatory and competitive business contexts. Deals were often done in the form of fees paid to recoup perceived loss of postal revenue in the face of intransigent legal and political positions and rising legal costs.

And What About This "Smuggling" Theory?

The other potential bottleneck in DHL's relentless quest for speed occurred, not surprisingly, at customs points of entry. As we have alluded to earlier, laws applicable to the import of goods were intent on protecting local industry and raising revenue from import duties. The process of ensuring ownership of imported goods, verifying contents and ensuring duties were paid, evolved into the emergence of agents acting on behalf of importers. These agents were licensed as customs brokers by the customs authorities themselves, and over time the desired arm's length relationship between customs officials and brokers blurred into questionable familiarity and questionable practice. Courier services presented a logistical problem to the players in this cosy relationship. Onboard couriers carrying many small items of little or no extrinsic commercial value usurped the brokers' exclusive rights to present the documentation to customs, seeking clearance. Thus it was not surprising that customs brokers proved to be a barrier to regulatory reform in pursuit of faster processing of time sensitive materials carried by DHL and other couriers, as well as supporting customs officials as willing partners to postal agencies' declarations of war on couriers' alleged breach of their monopoly. Breaches of customs processes and misrepresentation of content were eagerly pursued by customs and their broker partners in an effort to control the upstart DHL from upsetting their status quo.

And problems did indeed arise at customs, if not orchestrated by a zealous interpretation of a given law, then randomly through inspections, seizures or other methods of delay. Being exposed to random interventions at customs, was almost as bad as being stopped outright, because an extra hour consumed in customs had huge potential to disrupt delivery and pick-up schedules throughout the day, and there was never much margin for time slippage in a courier's schedule. Ostensibly, the problem was perception, as each consignment of DHL bags was declared, correctly, as documents having no commercial value, meaning of course extrinsic value, the value realized if the documents were sold. Fortunately, the arguments put forward in defense against alleged postal monopoly infringements, that the value was an intangible asset called time, never translated into an argument about customs duties. So, for the most part, a customs officer at the passenger arrival would make a cursory inspection, opening one or two, for example, out of twenty bags, take a good look at the courier (dress codes applied), and wave both courier and bags through. On the freight side, a similar process would unfold, and more often than not a quick inspection of the customs declaration would suffice. As computerized processes gradually took hold, consignments were often cleared in advance of arrival, unless a system of random selection was in play, and a DHL consignment was picked on any given day for detailed inspection. These interventions were accepted as an occasional risk to a routine process, and customers also became quite understanding of the unpredictability of an occasional customs intervention.

But, the core issue was trust, and trust is influenced by perception. Customs officers became used to the style and approach of DHL employees at the various clearance points, their enthusiasm, their integrity, and their generally cheerful disposition. The later concept of "known shipper" which has become a key indicator of trust by busy customs officials all round today's security conscious world was effectively applied in an earlier version to DHL, its couriers and employees. But that trust was always undermined, if indeed something other than a document was being carried, and was discovered. And that happened often! Customers would frequently, and for the most part innocently, send personal correspondence, cash, videos and other items which would stretch the most vivid imagination to be described as business documents. But the customers were as unfamiliar with the regulations as they were with the destination environment.

Take Saudi Arabia, for example. Opening up Saudi Arabia to customers was a huge boon to the young company's growth potential. The oil boom was like a gold rush; every country wanted a piece of the action, and so most countries had companies represented in Saudi Arabia doing or looking for business. But it was not an easy place to live, let alone do business in. Strict Islamic laws applied, commercial regulation was both unpredictable and bureaucratic, women could not drive or work, and alcohol was strictly forbidden. On top of that, the climate was harshly hot and dusty. It was easy to empathize with a mailroom employee in the customer's office in, say Houston, when someone wanted to send a little extra in the daily pouch to make life easier for a colleague or family member working in Riyadh. But that innocent act would often cause major problems at the end of the line, if a DHL employee in Saudi Arabia had to explain to an angry customs officer, who might occasionally discover a *Playboy* magazine in among the company mail. Pornography, as well as anything with a connection to the State of Israel, were anathema to Saudi authorities. Videos were a specific problem, as the only way to inspect was to confiscate and play. In such environments, especially if a breach of trust occurred, customs processes became more akin to a lottery, which further exacerbated the ability to maintain a consistent schedule of pick-ups and deliveries on the ground.

Because it was difficult, even in a fledgling global like DHL, to create at origin a common understanding of each country's idiosyncrasies and customs rules, DHL was forced to introduce its own checking processes at consolidation points. Many couriers in the early days were astute enough to spot problems early on, but rapid growth and a proliferation of destinations made precise knowledge at the point of pickup difficult to convey. So, at export or transfer points, shipments were checked for obvious bulk in any packages coming through, to see if content really complied with the no-commercial-value declaration, or to see if there were any obvious letters in the contents or to remove suspicious videos or suspect magazines. Unopened envelopes which had been through a domestic postal service, with the stamps still visible, were a case in point. Of course, customers would often become frustrated, if, for example, some other customer's material had caused a delay to their own compliant shipment. Or, they asked innocently, why can't DHL organize itself to carry such packages? This of course was a legitimate question, particularly for commercial goods, and as demand for express services grew, DHL was constantly telling customers no, they couldn't take this or that commercial sample, or this urgent spare part for repair. But saying no was not what made DHL successful in the first place!

In this context, DHL was becoming a victim of its own success, in that it had built its system of speed and reliability on a simple, if not insignificant niche: documents of no commercial value. So, while regulatory issues of a customs nature were not the biggest issue in the 70s, it certainly became so later, as DHL took its first uncertain steps of responding to customer demand to carry dutiable items, i.e., with a commercial value.

Airline Schizophrenia

Adding to the cauldron of the common cause which aligned postal authorities, customs and brokers, a separate battle waxed and waned with the commercial carriers, fair-weather friends of the upstart DHL. As seen earlier, the CAB in the USA had huge influence on the air transport industry, be it passenger or freight, and macro-economic reform, carried out by the Nixon and subsequently Carter administrations, progressively broke up this regulatory behemoth in favor of a more open skies, competitive environment. But in the 70s, the CAB ruled on just about everything, including the cost to the passenger of excess baggage. Hence airlines carrying passengers from the U.S., operated under a piece rate regime regardless of weight.

The airlines found themselves conflicted on several fronts in their dealings with DHL and other couriers. On the one hand, revenue and yield from selling a passenger ticket every day with no cost of sale was a very welcome addition to the product mix. On the other hand, piece rates provided, from their perspective, no disincentive to passengers bypassing the freight channel and carrying inordinate numbers of bags which clogged up the baggage carousels and annoyed other passengers. U.S. airlines in the 1970s, particularly the largest, Pan Am, introduced a new convention for defining and charging for excess baggage by pricing at the rate per kilogram equivalent to one percent of the first class airfare. (Interestingly, one of the early CAB rulings found that the actual costs of carrying excess baggage amounted to an equivalent kilogram tariff of 0.7 of the *economy* fare.) Other airlines internationally seized on this one percent convention and were not constrained by the regulatory oversight enjoyed by the CAB.

In the late 70s, DHL and other players became embroiled in a long running dispute with Pan Am, conducted through the regulatory process of Pan Am filing tariffs with the CAB and then DHL raising a complaint. DHL's arguments were for the most part rationally cost-based, but invariably linked with more subjective arguments which questioned the applicability of antiquated postal and customs laws, underpinned by Larry's visionary passion to transform the role of government to be a facilitator, not a controller, of international commerce. While this was essentially a commercial dispute, the debates which raged through the CAB process, provided useful precedents for the more commercial approaches to the issue of courier baggage which emerged in the 80s. As another example of Larry's determination as well as commercial foresight, if not guts, in the early battle with Pan Am, he acquired a small stake in the airline, which enabled him to attend shareholder meetings to point out the short-sightedness of Pan Am's predatory pricing practices. A few years later he was able to sell those shares for a huge profit when DHL badly needed the money. And, of course Pan Am, ultimately bankrupt, ended up losing the lucrative DHL business to competitors!

Putting aside the commercial considerations which perplexed the airlines in dealing with DHL as a new kind of customer, the key regulatory advantage which defined DHL's relationships with the airline industry were the flying and landing rights which governments bestowed on their national airlines. These rights were jealously guarded and negotiated with other civil aviation regimes as airlines sought to fly to and from foreign cities, acquiring the rights to land and take-off, at the same time dropping passengers off and picking up new ones for the return flight or onward to a third destination, in competition with the destination country's own national carrier. Rights to fly passengers also extended to rights to carry cargo. Not having a home base or dominant nationality was something which defined DHL to its advantage as a nascent global company, and it was a virtue as long as DHL had no ambitions to fly its own aircraft. It didn't have such ambitions in the early days, because it was unaffordable.

Thus, the schizophrenia which characterized relationships between DHL and the airlines in the 70s was caused by the uncertainty which the new business and business model created. Was DHL a valuable customer or a nuisance? Was it a threat? Would it try to become an airline (like FedEx)? Should we partner or compete with DHL? Should we treat DHL the same as or differently from its competitors? Pan Am's behavior in the 70s typified the confusion felt, and this situation was only clarified in later years when DHL clearly demonstrated its preference for partnerships as long as service commitments could thereby be met or improved.

Okay, Understand the Challenges With Post Offices, Customs and Airlines, But Surely You Were Doing Everything Else by the Book?

In those early days of frantic daily deadlines and breakneck expansion (in the first fifteen years, one new city every eight days; one new country every five weeks), compliance was not always a top priority for DHL's untrained business novices. Being appropriately incorporated, paying payroll taxes, and keeping a proper set of accounts was not the priority of a business driven by its customers to operate everywhere. In some countries, foreign exchange regulations were in force which meant that paying an overseas supplier was a nightmare of red tape if not corrupt practice. This issue would become more problematic in the 80s, but even in the early days of operating in what were, for the most part, developed jurisdictions, transferring surplus funds created problems. For example, in

France, the couriers flew in every day from London on tickets paid for in London. The customers sending from France were charged a single price for the entire service, but DHL France only paid to get the shipments to the airport. It didn't take long, therefore, for considerable cash to accumulate in the Paris bank account, and, while there were no foreign exchange restrictions, there still had to be a valid and logical rendering of an invoice to be approved by the transferring bank as legitimate. There were potential tax issues at stake, and in those days the terminology and concept of transfer pricing did not exist as a means of potentially avoiding tax in one jurisdiction in favor of paying in another, lower tax environment. This situation was a direct consequence of the novel operating principles which evolved earlier in the decade: keep it simple, one all-inclusive price, and consolidate through key transfer hubs to get scale. The situation in London was the obverse: although London was by far the biggest business unit in terms of inbound and outbound shipments, it was also a major transfer hub, and picked up most of the airline bills. London was always short of cash.

In fact, DHL was starting to generate a lot of cash, but it was often in the wrong places. Larry, with his futuristic perspective, was already worrying about the prospect of DHL's document courier business having a short life cycle in the face of emergent technologies. So how to deal with this conundrum of getting cash into the right jurisdictions, not to deliberately avoid tax, but purely to pay the bills and make the investments necessary to stay ahead of the game, became a serious issue.

Chapter 8
1970s Vignettes and Bloopers

By the end of the 70s, DHL had arrived, albeit still fragile, in the face of a business model so novel and so disruptive that the forces of reaction and regulatory obstinacy were assembling on many fronts. The spirit of the pioneer, that unique blend of attitudes and cultures which derived from the founders, the willingness to confront the odds, manage "by the seat of one's pants" and just work fearlessly hard, had gotten DHL this far. There were many heroics and subtle innovations, and there were a few things which went wrong, or didn't succeed, or were premature.

Strange Bedfellows

In the early days, bag and package transfer operations typically took place in any convenient spot, in carparks, in vacant lots, in airport arrival halls. There were either no facilities available, or DHL couldn't afford the rent. In Paris, the courier bags were unloaded in the Charles De Gaulle underground carpark, a place where prostitutes also plied their trade in parked cars. In New York, the airport office was like a cave beneath the Pan Am heliport, an open area containing one typewriter, one telex machine and a fish tank. No fun in the winter!

Caught Napping

In Bahrain, the airport office was actually on the airport tarmac, as the big Qantas jumbo jets arrived in the middle of the night, and DHL's local partner had managed to secure an airside pass. The airport operation in Bahrain was an all-night operation for the one or two guys assigned to effect the transfers in those early days. Being Australasians, they quickly formed collegial relations with the Qantas staff, such that a quick nap in a first class seat during a transit stop was a tempting possibility, provided of course you woke up and got off before the doors closed for take-off. Yes, it did happen, and one angry captain had to taxi back one night to let the scruffy overall-clad Kiwi off the plane.

https://doi.org/10.1515/9781501507557-011

Plenty of Space, and Not So Much

In Dubai, the sorting was done in the airport carpark, but that was ok because it rarely rained in the Middle East. In London, for a couple of years, the airport office was the loading bay at Trans World Airlines' (TWA) freight warehouse. More often than not, the roll-a-door was open, which meant that a few feet of warehouse, officially designated as in-bond, or in other words, across the border, would be available to spread things about. It also meant that at the last minute, a DHL courier with a green bag or two hoisted on his shoulders, could be seen running through the warehouse and onto the tarmac to throw the bags onto the TWA truck heading for the plane. Conversely, and mostly during inclement weather common in London, if the door was closed, the DHL team had a scarce eighteen inches of space to do the manifesting and courier delivery sheets while trying to keep everything dry!

Strange Passengers

Going back to the Middle East, Bahrain was the transit hub and the biggest market was Saudi Arabia. The biggest destination in Saudi was Dhahran, Dammam and Al Khobar, two adjacent urban sprawls just across the water from Bahrain. Nowadays one can drive there across a causeway, but back then it was a ten-minute flight on a Fokker 27 (F27), a small but reliable passenger plane which took off every hour from Bahrain across the channel. These planes carried little freight, so the solution was to buy four seats on every flight, with the bags strapped into seats as passengers, along with the Bahraini national courier, who didn't require a visa. Or sometimes without the courier, because his seat was needed by the bags. Never mind! The documents always got through, sometimes to the bemusement if not frustration of the customers themselves, who might have been traveling on related business but unable to get a seat because of the green bag couriers.

Delivery Heroics

Heroics also took place in the busy central business districts of the big cities. In London, for example, many was the time that a fresh-faced colonial recruit was thrust into London traffic with a load of deliveries (twenty to thirty) all across the vast city, only days after having arrived in the UK for a holiday. But at least the streets had names, the maps were readable, and the language was English. Those same couriers often had to set off to Europe to do several cities in one day, with maps which, although accurate, were in French or German. And they drove on the wrong side of the road! Luxury, that same courier would reflect, when he landed in Riyadh, where there were no maps, and no street names, and all available signs were in Arabic. There were also no GPS systems, no mobile phones, no Google Maps, thus each courier was obliged to use up precious time irritating customers with requests to use the phone to call back to the office to announce success, failure, or whether there were any "special" pickups to be added to the day's route. Every day bore witness to such dedicated, dogged determination to complete the day's work. And if things got delayed, and deliveries were missed, they were invariably taken home and the courier would set out extra early the next morning to complete the route.

In Tokyo, the street addresses were by building number, and in the order the buildings were built. There was therefore no logic for the early pioneers (two Japanese Americans) to follow. Each block had to be mastered through dogged familiarization, which they often did at night.

In Hong Kong, the problem was a different one; density of buildings in narrow streets made it difficult to drive, and so couriers had walking routes, supported by a bus which did a circular route. The bus also functioned as a mobile sorting office with couriers popping up from the street throwing bags on board and receiving the next load of deliveries. When the MTR (Hong Kong's underground train service) commenced operations, the train replaced the bus, with a courier permanently riding a loop and bags being thrown across the gates at the various stations during stops. Only one train ticket per day!

It's Tough Being Ahead of Your Time

But it was galling to be so dedicated to customer service, to be able to find someone at a moment's notice to go to a new country and set up from scratch, to constantly delight customers with an unbelievable transit time, yet have to say no when asked to send dutiables. Toward the end of the 70s, the demand to send small parcels of a varied, but commercial nature, became a crescendo of queries, more pleading than frustrated, from customers who couldn't get the same commitment to speed from their freight forwarder.

And so it was that one station manager, on a routine pick up call to an oil service customer in Dubai, was asked if DHL could get a key piece of drilling equipment to Houston for repair and return. Not wanting to say no, and having heard on the DHL grapevine that parcels were the next big thing, the package was accepted and a call was made to Bahrain to ask if it could be done. The answer came back yes (of course) but don't send it through London—get it to Singapore and ask them to send it to enter the U.S. via Honolulu, where customs relations were perceived to be more flexible. So off the package went, without any customs paperwork, just as if it were a document, but with telex instructions to the transfer point. Into the DHL ether!

Exactly a week later, the package arrived back in Dubai, to the station manager's astonished delight. But alas, upon closer inspection it was the same package which had left a week before, but with a lot of marker pen all over it. The folks in Honolulu had scrawled, "We don't do parcels; send this back to THR" (THR is Tehran, Iran, not DXB, Dubai, United Arab Emirates). Below that scrawl the manager in Tehran had cryptically added "do not send to THR either, send to DXB" and promptly re-dispatched the package. Tehran was serviced by courier and freight from London, so the package had gone from Dubai to Bahrain to Singapore, to Honolulu, to London, to Tehran, back to London, to Bahrain and then Dubai, all in the space of a calendar week. It had no doubt cleared customs several times illegally, but, critically, DHL had failed to live up to its "nothing's a problem" credo. It was a very sheepish Dubai manager who delivered the package back to the customer, with a huge "FAIL" mark. Fortunately, the customer was accustomed to such things happening, and the account was not lost, but the point was telling: How on earth was DHL to learn the parcels business, when its very existence to date was to concentrate on doing the simple stuff well, and avoid the complexity of customs regulations and customs duties? This was one of the major challenges of the 80s, and one which could not be described as overcome until the 90s.

Another failure, or perhaps more kindly interpreted as another premature effort, was in the area of computing. As mentioned earlier, there were no computers commercially available to small or start-up businesses in the early 70s. Technology was limited to the electric typewriter and the telex machine. International phone calls were often unreliable, and always expensive. DHL's fast courier service was an effective substitute for all but the most critically urgent messages and information. But by the mid-70s, commercial facsimile machines began to appear, as did word processors (the precursor to the PC) focused on document creation and storage. The prospect of smarter technology, both creating and communicating content electronically, was a concern to Larry, who saw it as a real threat. So he embarked on another venture, to build a word processor which could anticipate the internet as a means of transmitting documents electronically. Concurrently, he conceived of a super fax machine which could act as an electronic carrier, substituting the plane as a physical carrier which could be strategically located in DHL offices around the world, and act as a receiving bureau for printing and last mile physical delivery. A lot of cash went into the design and manufacture of these DHL 1000 word processors, as they were known. Recognizing the importance of the Middle East to DHL's success to date, an Arabic language version was also created, which was a world first. The fax idea ended up being a costly diversion from the core business. On the word processing front, Wang had more marketing capability (DHL was certainly not a marketing company) and Apple was making its first moves.

And ultimately the fax turned out to be a facilitator for growth, neither a threat nor a substitute. Larry was both right and wrong here: he was right in terms of future trends, but he was wrong on the timing. The silver lining was that the early DHL leaders, who were operators, neither marketers nor technologists, got an early feel for how important technology was about to become, not just in their own core business, but to the world of globalization, which was about to take off.

Chapter 9
Transition

Taken Off, but Not Yet Landed

By the end of the 70s, DHL had arrived, precariously, as a company able to survive the turbulent start-up years, and had confronted, if not overcome, most of the barriers which could be conceived when creating something novel and new. The one thing absent was effective competition. Sure, there were competitors; some attempted to emulate DHL's rapid global reach and failed, or were acquired by bigger competitors who emerged more effectively in the 80s. And there were the U.S. giants, FedEx and UPS, each larger by far than all of DHL put together, but domestically focused. They would emerge as forces to be reckoned with in the following decade.

The first existential threat to DHL came from a competitor whistleblowing to a regulatory agency. An early example of how regulation stimulates rent-seeking (gaining advantage through lobbying or the manipulation of public policy) and/or crony capitalism seen in modern day dictatorships. Loomis began earlier in the century as an armored car business, along with Purolator (Pure Oil Later) a filter company which acquired a Canadian courier business. Neither of DHL's early competitors saw the mail courier business as a prime opportunity, and soon faded from the scene. Interestingly, both brands have re-emerged in Canada, having gone through numerous corporate upheavals.

DHL's real competition in the 70s emerged from an unlikely, but not surprising, source. Australian domestic operators Thomas Nationwide Transport (TNT, which then acquired Alltrans) and IPEC (Interstate Parcel Express Company) became early adopters of the principle of integration, both vertical (i.e. door-to-door, cut out the middleman) and horizontal, or across all modes of transport. These two businesses, which ultimately came together in the 80s, were run by global entrepreneurs Sir Peter Abeles and Gordon Barton who competed and collaborated over the coming years with DHL to advance the industry cause. The not-surprising element of this effort from Australia comes from both the practical logistics of moving goods across a vast, underpopulated continent, along with the common pioneering culture of the colonial which shaped a large part of DHL's growth.

Another threat emerged in the form of Calico, a DHL emulator owned by an American friend of Dave Allen. Calico followed DHL's global expansion as quickly as it could and even pre-empted DHL by getting a foothold in the Middle

https://doi.org/10.1515/9781501507557-012

East. Brown & Root, one of DHL's earliest customers, surprised the DHL management in London in early 1976 by demanding service to Bahrain or else they would use this "someone else." DHL opened in Bahrain in a matter of weeks. We have seen earlier how much impact being able to service the Middle East had on DHL's growth and market leadership elsewhere, so the Brown and Root ultimatum proved to be fortuitous.

And in various parts of the world, especially UK and Europe, extant or opportunistic specialist operators focusing on a specific sector or geographic niche provided important, but ultimately nuisance, value stimulus to DHL's unquestioned leadership and thirst for global growth.

But by 1979, the Australian threat was still in its infancy, Calico's customer list was acquired by DHL (as was that of Securicor, another security focused company in the UK), Federal Express was just getting its head above water in its chosen domestic U.S. niche, and UPS kept on domestically trucking.

DHL's position as a global leader was established, but far from recognized, as the DHL brand still had no generic association with what was being done, and the regulatory battles were far from won. Hence the "arrival" was indeed precarious.

A Biological Phenomenon

Perhaps because of that lack of an effective global competitor, perhaps because of the regulatory hiccups, which forced the separation of DHL into separate fiscal entities, perhaps because all available time was spent on building a global network, DHL ended the first ten years of its life essentially headless. There was no head office, no single CEO, no structure, no process, no formulated and formal strategy on how to deal with the issues, how to continue to finance growth, or how to survive. How do you categorize a body without a head?

"Emergent" is one answer, using the term as applied in philosophy, systems theory, science and art, whereby larger entities arise through interactions among smaller or simpler entities such that the larger entities exhibit properties the smaller/simpler entities do not or cannot exhibit.

Steven Johnson, in his popular science book, *Emergence: The Connected Lives of Ants, Brains, Cities, and Software*, describes emergent systems as:

adaptive self-organizing systems: systems that are made up of many interacting agents who are individually not terribly smart, but who collectively come up with intelligent higher-level behavior. An ant colony is a great example of this kind of system.[1]

Just as ants, seemingly intuitively, find the shortest distance to a food source, without any apparent leadership, other systems build scale and intelligence in natural as opposed to artificial ways. Examples such as the formation of city neighborhoods, or the response of our immune systems, or collaborative software writing all point to this phenomenon.

Does it make sense to describe DHL, a courier service engaged in the not-so-sexy delivery of time-sensitive documents between major cities worldwide, as a prime example of this sphere of thought?

Po Chung thinks so:

> Viewed a certain way, you could even say that our company was optimizing itself, by leveraging local, disconnected points of knowledge to expanding into an international network. The term for this phenomenon is *emergence*, where a system emerges from simpler constituent parts. The amazing thing is that we didn't actively plan for it to be that way–for local points of contact to feed into a distributed trans-national business system. All we did was approach our business flexibly, and lay down the constituent parts–our values and our practices.

Growth in the DHL network was exponential. Adding a new country or city to the network multiplied the options for service exponentially. It was customer driven and it was opportunistic; there was no detailed, structured plan. And because of geographical diversity, it was not an orderly, symmetrical picture. In contrast, Federal Express' growth within a domestic USA context was structured; the idea emerged from Fred Smith's college thesis, and the central hub-and-spoke formula spoke of order, efficiency and symmetry, much like a spider spinning its web. DHL's web looked more like, and perhaps foreshadowed, the worldwide web of the internet, chaotic and disorderly. But it worked, day in, day out, and grew at a tremendous pace. Perhaps a spider's web without the spider? Or hundreds of spiders working away at the same web independently, but connected?

---

1 Johnson, Steven. *Emergence: The Connected Lives of Ants, Brains, Cities, and Software.* New York: Scribner, 2002.

With Intuitive, Instinctive Leadership

The insect analogy has probably run its course, and we can avoid offending our colleagues who participated in the phenomena of DHL's emergence by making a further comparison to today's artificial intelligence world. In this world, systems are designed, then design themselves into self-learning entities. DHL's version of this arose, more by accident than design, from the opposing realities of insatiable demand for more service and more destinations; and increasingly implacable and organized opposition from the regulatory authorities. DHL had no leaders in a corporate structure sense, partly because its owner leaders were in a fight for the right to exist which was also, incidentally, a fight for industry recognition and survival. But partly also because of the practicalities of managing rapid growth.

Young managers out in the frontline knew more about the detail of the postal monopolies than they knew about the finances of their business. And they had to take decisions on the spot, in real time, to ensure operational continuity and consistency.

Couriers knew more about their customer's business than they ostensibly knew about their own. What they were intuitively doing was building their business from the bottom up, both in terms of ensuring operational consistency, but also in terms of knowledge. Knowledge of customers, knowledge of local customs (in contrast to, but as well as, local customs regulations) and knowledge of what worked locally, to achieve the same outcome as was achieved elsewhere, but perhaps done differently. Hence there was considerable divergence in operating procedures, albeit in a homogenous context: you organized locally to pick-up, export, clear and deliver. It was all about the outcome, not the method, the what, not the how.

Hence you might rationalize, with the benefit of hindsight that chaos versus order was an existential virtue, if not a necessity. Exponential growth and orderly, structured decision making are incompatible realities. But of course, that is a little unkind to the owners and early leaders who were in place to hire, to sell, to organize, to trouble shoot, and get the business through each frantic day. And more: to work out which country next, to resource and finance that effort, and to design and implement the most effective mode of air transport and routing to service the tangled web. In other words, optimize the flow, as we shall further discuss. Even in the appearance of chaos, there is arguably natural order.

The problem was twofold: first, none of these managers had formal corporate experience or much if any business training. Second, the visionary leaders were largely pre-occupied with survival against the perception of being illegal everywhere. So, while there was no corporate leadership to speak of, there was *heroic operational leadership*, and *fearless industry leadership* at play here. It is even wrong to speak of industry leadership in any other than nascent terms, because there was no industry. There was a business concept which the authorities wanted to strangle at birth. And there were a handful of players more intent on strangling each other than combining forces for their common industry good. DHL alone, stood out from all the rest in carrying the burden of regulatory reform in these formative, emergent years. This, one might argue, was a consequence of Larry's iconoclast nature; but iconoclast with a vision of a world where governments promoted rather than restricted free trade. Larry wasn't alone in this, but certainly in the minority, and at the forefront of the great global deregulation which occurred in the subsequent two decades.

Which Attracted and Inspired

If more by instinct than by design, the founders soon sensed that they couldn't control what they had started with a centralized, top-down view of the world. And they saw that they were attracting a cadre of employees who reveled in the pace, the excitement and the challenges which were being faced on a daily basis. All around the world people were standing up to be counted, and even if they weren't being counted, that didn't stop their daily, heroic performances of dealing with flight delays, random customs holdups and traffic jams as mere irritants in the process of fulfilling the customer promise.

Those that were counted rose quickly through the managerial ranks, and the core values associated with being a courier were covertly institutionalized as a consequence. Those that missed out need not wait long for the next opportunity, if indeed that was what they were after, because there was always another opportunity not too far down the road. There was no greater illustration of this than in London, the largest single city, or station in the network, and the base from which expansion into Europe, the Middle East and Africa took place. Dave Allen initially recruited through the London rugby clubs where he found former playing mates from Sydney, and other former colonies such as New Zealand and to a lesser extent Zimbabwe (then Rhodesia). Throw in the occasional South African or two, and the occasional Brit, and you had a decidedly colonial, Anglo-Saxon cadre who happened to be in London, and available. They were there as a result of the great exodus, or rite of passage, which characterized young people's desire to escape from their relatively isolated and restricted home countries' environments. Most of these young people were off on their OE (overseas experience) for a year or two; the length of time for which a work visa was readily available, or for which funds were available, for which a parental leave pass had been negotiated. When the rugby club recruiting avenue periodically ran dry, jobs were advertised, not in the local press, but in Australia or New Zealand House, where these countries' high commissions were located.

Cowboys with Wing

In those mid 70s days, DHL might well have been perceived as fly-by-night, meant in the unflattering context, but Dave's cowboys didn't care. It didn't matter. If it all ended suddenly one day, you could just go home. And besides, while it lasted, and if you carried your passport on you, at any moment you might be excused the challenges of London's traffic and be asked to fly off somewhere to deliver a "special," a shipment so urgent that customers were prepared to pay the full cost of a bespoke service. And, if you were within shouting distance, when Dave arrived at the office to announce that Citibank wanted services to six European cities within three weeks, and he said: "of course"; then you might be asked to pack a bag and leave that night to start up a new office in a new city in a new country. All of a sudden, the London overseas experience, where you worked at any job, no matter how menial, became a global one with travel and accommodation and a decent wage on top!

And an Ounce of Luck

And so when Brown & Root threatened to use Calico if DHL couldn't provide service to Bahrain, service to the Middle East was initiated. But in this context, you might also ask:

> The global oil crisis is fueling an exploration extravaganza. The Middle East has rapidly become a focal point of world commerce and is ill-equipped to manage its communication needs with the rest of the world. And DHL is there with its restless generation of young expatriates, based in London, who provide a mobile, articulate, fearless, young workforce. You have a product or service which takes off in the most inhospitable of environments, facing existential regulatory threats, and you put all this together, and suddenly own this burgeoning marketplace, how lucky is that?

Well that depends on how you define luck, and even the most bullish exponents of DHL would acknowledge the role of luck along the way. The Middle East phenomena is also not to be overstated as similar situations elsewhere in the world have already played out, or are yet to be played out. After all, success in the Middle East provided impetus and momentum, not a raison d'etre. But it does illustrate the relevance of the concept of emergence: turbulence in global trade, triggered by the oil crisis drove new commercial imperatives to open up new markets, quickly. A new, disruptive corporate endeavor emerged as a result, creating new value propositions such as speed to market, the value of time, the importance of simplicity, the power of disintermediation and integration. A global upstart.

Underpinned by Trust

Trust and pride are other phenomena to be acknowledged here. The impracticality of command and control as a corporate approach meant that freedom to act was the necessary alternative. And if not deliberate, implicit trust was an early feature of the way DHL worked. At a macro level, it was the trust in your counterpart on the other side of the world to fulfill the promise made to a local customer. At a micro level, it was the trust conveyed to the courier that the relationship with the customer was one which they "owned." And all over the world it was the trust that in the face of a crisis, the person on the spot was best positioned to make a decision, and begging forgiveness is a better outcome if things go wrong than seeking permission beforehand. Trust resulted universally in increased responsibility and accountability for the problem at hand. As a result, DHL people were proud of what they were achieving, to the point where they felt they owned the business themselves.

A Common Language

DHL's early culture was largely defined by its Anglo-Saxon heritage and English as the common language (counting Hong Kong as Anglo-Saxon in this context). Diversity did indeed exist between the U.S., UK and Asia versions of the culture, but the common language allowed nuance and enthusiasm to be more easily communicated across the world. This is important. The move toward a service economy and a service mindset requires an ability to communicate both factually and emotionally. A service is only a service if the provider and receiver unite in a moment of mutual benefit which involves an emotional connection, even if physically separate. Proficiency in the English language and the emergence of a common DHL language enabled the nuances of communication which enhance a service experience, and certainly helped DHL spread its message across diverse cultures and languages. But it wasn't just the language. The English speaking cultures also had common ground in terms of their legal codes, and it is in this combination of common language and common legal and commercial principles that the terms maritime versus continental are better understood.

And the Rule of Common Law

Typically, the maritime countries have a legal code based on English law, deriving from the thirteenth century, in contrast to the continental European framework which derives from the Napoleonic Code introduced in the early nineteenth century, and adopted or adapted extensively throughout much of the rest of the world. In simple terms, the English common law system is based on legal precedent, which builds up over time (case law). Bottom up. Napoleonic civil law attempts to codify acceptable behavior by statute. Top down. The presumption in English law is of innocence. In contrast, the presumption in Napoleonic law is of guilt. The more liberal framework of common law has arguably been better in supporting the emergence of global service players, versus, for instance, manufacturing, where global excellence has been more evident from continental, or civil law frameworks. Could DHL have emerged from continental Europe or Japan? Hard to say. But the majority of the DHL people who played on their luck in the face of regulatory hurdles, and who had great respect for as well as ability to inspire diverse cultures, in direct contrast to their disrespect for rules, were clearly more "maritime" than "continental" in origin and mindset.

Putting all these considerations to one side, what can be more unequivocally said about the nature of DHL in 1979 as an emerging global giant?

First, it had a great product, which was valued everywhere. Second, it was innovative and disruptive to the point of being at risk of premature extinction. Third, absent any substitute technology, it relied almost exclusively on people to perform, in local situations, a global service. Fourth, those employees had instilled in them, implicitly if not explicitly, the values of the entrepreneurial founders, a synthesis of the best of each of them. And finally there was trust, in each other, in the product, and in the belief that performing the DHL service was the right thing to do. Trust was the glue which substituted for rules and standard operating procedures.

But it was Precarious

The most extraordinary thing of all about DHL's arrival at the cusp of the 80s was that fact that it had survived its first ten years without external capital or debt. In contrast, Federal Express was started in 1974 with what was at the time record venture capital funding of $91 million. Obviously, the artistic nature of the pricing construct and level of pricing developed at the outset had some basis in fact. For no doubt the margins were there, given the self-generation of cash for expansion and the somewhat odd diversification efforts as well!

But that cash was often in the wrong place, and no one knew anyway precisely where and how much it was. There was no budgeting, no cash management, no capital controls, no strategic plan. The absence of clear guidelines, if not rules on how organize and sustain what was by now a large business was causing friction and unproductive noise among the handful of headstrong "leaders" operating across Europe, US and the Middle East.

Larry and his shareholder colleagues knew that the loose, bottom up approach which had seen the organization through the first frantic decade of explosive growth needed some counterbalancing order from a central, global perspective. As unified as the network was on the core functions of pick-up and delivery, there was increasing divergence between countries and their pseudo regional groupings from which individual leadership voices emerged. It was in effect a grouping of local entities struggling with the concept, as well as the reality, of being a global business in nature.

And the Australians were biting and the U.S. (relative) giants were nibbling jealously at DHL's success.

Something had to be done to sustain the business, as well as maintain the special nature of what had been achieved in terms of emerging culture and leadership.

Chapter 10
The 80s

Economic and Political Turbulence...

The 70s decade closed with the onset of a global recession that gripped the developed world in the early 80s. Inflationary pressure not seen before (20 percent interest rates in the U.S. in 1980) caused a rethink and a revival of laissez-faire economics with a focus on deregulation, less government intervention and lower taxes. The failed economic policies of the late 70s would take a while to unwind, but the world was ready for change. The "supply-side Reaganomics" response along with the globalization effects discussed in this chapter, drove the federal funds rate down to 6 percent in 1987. Another small but significant example is New Zealand, virtually bankrupt after decades of protectionist economic policy, which moved in three short years, 1984-7, from being the most highly regulated economy in the OECD (Organisation for Economic Co-operation and Development) bloc, to being the most deregulated. On the other hand, many developing (or so-called Third World) countries suffered downstream, and debt crisis followed debt crisis with multiple interventions and prescriptive assistance required from the International Monetary Fund.

Presaging Fundamental Geopolitical Change

Ronald Reagan became president of the USA, and oversaw the re-emergence of America as an uncompromising global power pursuing capitalism as a holy crusade, rejecting the 70s détente philosophy of the Nixon/Kissinger era and challenging the Soviet bear politically and militarily. In parallel if not in partnership, Margaret Thatcher became prime minister of Great Britain and resolutely tackled the industrial malaise that characterized the 70s, by taking on the powerful miners' union and pursuing a similar economic line of shrinking government and unshackling commerce. The economic battle lines were drawn, capitalism versus communism/socialism. The geopolitical context here was also a sense of Soviet vulnerability in the face of rising nationalism among its union members, especially Eastern European, and a messy entanglement in Afghanistan which exposed the myth of Soviet military prowess. Economically also, the five-year planning cycles embraced by the communist regimes were clearly not delivering, and as a result Mikhail Gorbachev as general secretary, began what was ultimately a

https://doi.org/10.1515/9781501597557-013

futile attempt to restructure the Russian and Soviet economy, without relaxing political power.

The Polish trade union, Solidarity, and its leader Lech Walesa, became household names across Europe and the world followed the Gdansk shipyard strikes in the summer of 1980. Other strikes followed across the country. In August, the government capitulated and Solidarity became an independent trade union. The government gradually reasserted its power and imposed martial law in December 1981, ending Poland's brief encounter with people power. But the seeds had been sown for later.

In 1981, Greece became the tenth member of the EU and Spain and Portugal followed five years later. In 1986, the Single European Act was signed. This is a treaty which provided the basis for a vast six-year program aimed at sorting out the problems with the free-flow of trade across EU borders and thus created the "single market." Deregulation became a buzzword, and one of the major initiatives worldwide, initially in the USA and UK, was to break up the telecommunications monopolies, or at least start that process by disentangling "telecommunications" from the "post" as occurred in the UK. This heralded a huge upswing in the use of telecommunications as costs inevitably came down as a result of more intense competition.

Policed by America

Both the U.S. and UK flexed military muscle during the 80s, with the UK responding to Argentina's takeover of the Falklands in 1982 in uncompromising fashion, and America showed a willingness to engage anywhere in the world if local wars or terrorism threatened its citizens and assets. Notable interventions occurred in Central America (Grenada, El Salvador) and the Middle East (in Lebanon, Libya, Persian Gulf). Behind the scenes the U.S. was active in supporting various Afghan factions in their struggle against the Soviet Union, Iraq in its decade long war with Iran, and of course Israel in its existential struggle in the Middle East. This is indeed the decade of Uncle Sam, the global policeman. And no matter how you view this from a national perspective, the 80s ends up a decade characterized by local and civil rather than regional or global conflicts.

With Asia Awakening

Economically, the Asian Tigers began to overtly demonstrate their emergence as a new economic block based on competition to provide lower cost for developed nations' manufacturing activities and in turn to learn from those imported skills to develop their own manufacturing base. Japan had shown the way in the 70s, with its focus on what was to be known as "just-in-time." Korea, Taiwan, Hong Kong (as the predominant gateways to China) and Singapore were early leaders in this great leap forward, followed by their smaller (in economic terms) rivals in the south east, Malaysia, Thailand and Indonesia. And China began to show it could reform economically without compromising its political control, unlike its Russian counterpart. The Chinese simply had more commercial DNA than the Russians, as demonstrated by the overseas Chinese dominance in the developing economies of Southeast Asia.

Business Models Must Change

This is the decade multi-national businesses changed their business models from being home country-dominant in terms of producing product, and international in terms of distribution, to being distributed on a global scale to take advantage of lower cost labor, raw materials and other incentives offered by developing countries in Asia, and elsewhere such as Mexico. These multinationals were predominantly U.S. companies, but also Japan, West Germany, UK and France saw economic revival in moribund home markets bolstered by international activity of their biggest commercial enterprises. Globalization was under way, and the 80s saw for the first time, transpacific trade equaling that of transatlantic trade, with America geographically in the middle, with its maritime perspective driving and benefiting from both trends. This multi-directional trend in trade patterns only served to solidify American economic power.

A New Age of Consumerism

Thus this became the decade when the *babyboomers*, that generational bubble which occurred as the western world re-populated after World War II, had come of age, unshackled from the conservative constraints of their war-weary parents, and started to consume like never before. And it was an exciting decade as the digital revolution took off. Every month or so some cool new technology appeared on the market. Personal computers were at the forefront, complemented or supported by new graphical user interfaces, and other consumer electronics such as the VCR, Walkman, camcorder, video games, cell and portable phones, answering machines, fax machines, CDs and an astonishing explosion in televised media and content, made possible by cable TV. By the mid-80s, 70 percent of the

American population had cable television! Time and time again, a new method of distribution, making things easier for consumers to access, use and buy, led to an explosion in demand.

Looking back on the 80s from a twenty-first century perspective it is not hard to reminisce nostalgically about an era of unremitting fun, a repeat of the 60s, but with technological rather than chemical toys to play with. And it was a decade without the ubiquity of real time communications which the age of the internet and mobile telephony unleashed in the subsequent decades. At work, business processes were comparatively simple, and long lunches ruled!

But, of course, the decade had a dark side: advantages in distribution also enabled huge cross-border flows in illicit drugs, notably cocaine, and the so-called war on drugs only served to strengthen and sophisticate the supply chains. Once again, a new method of distribution, making things easier for consumers to access, use and buy, led to an explosion in demand.

The permissiveness which access to drugs promoted in terms of uninhibited social behaviors also fueled a global AIDS epidemic which predominantly affected the gay community. Globalization in the form of easier and cheaper travel options on the one hand supported business growth, but it also enabled a faster spread of such a disease. Despite such setbacks to improved healthcare and longer life, significant technological advances also occurred which drove increased and more knowledgeable demand for personal healthcare. Surrogate births and the beginnings of genetic modification techniques appeared during the 80s.

And Speed to Market

It seemed like everything was getting faster and faster, and while both the USA and United Kingdom enjoyed a resurgence in global power, globalization this time around was a more distributed, shared phenomenon, not one dominated by a few. Companies from all around the world were moving out of home bases and establishing footholds in distant markets. In particular the Japanese companies, like Toyota, Honda, Sony, and Hitachi sprang up on their way to becoming household names throughout the western world. Business was on the move, whether it was a matter of decentralizing and distributing the supply chain, and expanding to embrace procurement as well as fulfillment, or whether it was a matter of getting a share of construction booms which accompanied economic growth in all country sectors, be they developed, developing or third world.

Whether it was a service expertise which was being exported into foreign markets, or an extraction capability—mining or drilling for natural resources—

the move was on. Business models needed to change and adapt in the face of such internationalization and globalization; lines of communication needed to be designed and implemented, and some of the new technologies were still very expensive. And regulatory environments were still predominantly in protectionist mode, in spite of visionary efforts by leading economies to break down barriers to trade. It was a bilateral and increasingly multilateral exercise; relaxing your own rules didn't work for long if your trade partners' and customers' rules didn't change also. Tariff and non-tariff barriers, such as a ban on foreign direct investment in a given service sector still predominated, and acquiring an understanding of how to manage access through one country's trade barriers didn't necessarily translate into experience which could be reused elsewhere. On the whole, doing business globally was still not for the faint- hearted! New services were required to help get things around, to help communications between overseas branches, to demystify complex customs processes, and to do so between any two points on the globe.

In 1979, a few enlightened customers might say, "thank goodness for DHL," but most didn't even know the name of the company which routinely surprised by delivering urgent documents in a phenomenally short timeframe.

In 1981, however, at the beginning of the decade which progressively embraced globalization as a force for good, Prime Minister Margaret Thatcher deregulated the British postal monopoly, and DHL, by launching its first ever television campaign, told the world the next day it was legitimately in business.

The End of History?

Fast forward to 1989 and Gorbachev's perestroika policy was as increasingly alien to many of the older communist regimes as it was appealing to their populations. East Germany's ruling elite panicked and opened up the Berlin Wall a symbolic but definitive signaling of the imminent collapse of the Soviet Union and an unequivocal response to the defining question of the twentieth century: communism or capitalism?

The question then became: what form of capitalism? The choice in those early, heady years when globalization became a force for good was between three distinct and coincidentally regional models. First, the stock-market driven jungle which was the United States, with its emphasis on meeting the quarterly numbers; or the oligopolistic variant found in Europe, with economic power concentrated in old moneyed organizations whose power was constrained only by the solidarity principles embodied in the German guild movement of the nineteenth century. Or, finally, the emerging Asian version with its blend of Confucianism and western principles and an emphasis on family values. In those days, the jury was out on whether the Asian model could survive the third-generational degeneration when too many grandchildren struggled to maintain the cohesion and strength of vision and commitment of their founding grandparent. And many despaired at the short-termism of the American approach with its apparent disincentive for long-term strategic thinking and action. Oligopolies similarly didn't pass muster in terms of public appeal, with the implied constraints to social mobility.

Perhaps a Hybrid Would be the Answer

At the beginning of the 80s, DHL was struggling from childhood to adolescence, and had not yet formed any composed idea of what it was or stood for. By the end of the decade DHL could stand tall and mature, and if not articulated in such terms, indeed represented a hybrid representation of those diverse traits of capitalism. A business that cared about its customers and its people, and acted like a big global family; a business which was also egalitarian and informal, priding itself on internal mobility; and a business which knew its numbers. A business which had a unique form, nationless but networked, and a set of values which transcended national boundaries and stereotypes, united in trust and commitment to service of the highest quality. A business driven by its customers, aware of and using the power of information technology, and "arrived" in the sense that it had attained global legitimacy in the face of seemingly impossible barriers. No longer a start-up, no longer an upstart, no longer barely legal, and now investor-ready.

But there is more of the story to tell.

Chapter 11
The Walden Years—Structure and Process

By 1979, DHL had service to over 200 cities in 48 countries and a turnover in excess of $100m. And this had been achieved without a clear plan supporting the Founders' vision, and without requiring external capital. This in itself was a remarkable achievement, driven by the determination of the founders and supported by a cadre of enthusiastic and passionate employees who worked as if the business were their own.

Nascently Global

But was it a global company? In the late 70s, there was very little if any debate about what it meant to go global, and what preconditions were required to be considered global. The definition of multinational seemed to start at doing business in more than one country. The *Harvard Business Review*, in reviewing a new book, *The Myth of the Global Corporation*[1] took a critical view of the concept, but not until 1998. The pertinent question from that review is: "Are we seeing the emergence of rootless corporations guided only by market opportunities, not by allegiance to their home countries?" There was nothing mythical in what DHL was achieving without a home base!

In 1979, DHL had no head office, no central planning, guidance, direction. No policies or standard operating procedure with perhaps the exception being the return of the POD slip. No budgets, no coordinated cash flows, no controls on capital expenditure. Critically, it had no nationality. Yes it was American at birth, with an iconoclastic view of the world typical of the American entrepreneur. But it didn't have common ownership; in fact, it was required to divest as part of the regulatory settlement with the CAB at the start of the decade. For sure, Larry had significant influence, but he certainly wasn't overtly in charge, setting goals, objectives, policies, hiring, firing, organizing. That wasn't his style or predisposition; he worked through and behind others. DHL Corporation, the US Company, was the largest business unit, but barely one-third of global turnover. And the number of DHL Corporation employees leading the charge internationally was

---

1 *The Myth of the Global Corporation*, Doremus, Keller, Pauly and Reich, Princeton University Press 1998.

https://doi.org/10.1515/9781501507557-014

virtually zero. So for sure, DHL, at the end of the 70s was decidedly not a U.S. multinational. So, what was it, if not a nascent global?

The more common view of a global company was one that traded everywhere, but with a dominant home base culture. And in the first big wave of globalization, in the late nineteenth and early twentieth centuries, the number of countries involved were few, and engaged in empire building. The globalization which kicked off in the late 70s, and gained traction in the 80s, involved many more countries. In fact, anyone could get involved, unless that country was still constrained by colonial or hegemonic relationships, notably the Eastern European bloc. So then the language shifted to multinational, with the underlying assumption that nationality was the key factor here in terms of the scope, the activity and the style of a given company operating in more than one country. And the fact that head office resided in the home country was surely a given. The predominant multinational mindset was more likely to be "act locally, globally." In other words, "what we do at home is what we will do everywhere."

DHL countries, on the other hand, absent any dominant culture or head office, were obliged if not encouraged to act local but think global; in other words, do what needs to be done locally to provide a globally homogenous service. Treating customers as one does in the USA or Japan will simply not work in France, unless the customer is American or Japanese. On the other hand, understanding and learning how from a French cultural perspective to deal with a Japanese company was indeed a small but important facet of the perceived benefits of globalization, namely the breaking down of cultural as well as trade barriers. It is premature to suggest DHL had these issues covered by 1979, but not implausible to suggest that the groundwork was underway.

Yes, there was a skein of common values and heritage driven by the English language dominance, and the predominately Anglo-Saxon nature of the international pioneers. But this was more of an expatriate culture than a specifically national one, and, relatively speaking, transient in the scheme of things. Not to underestimate the contribution of these people, some of whom went on to serve ten, twenty, even (recently) forty-year careers, but for the most part these characters spent two to five years on an overseas adventure and then went home. Like a shot of adrenaline to keep the headless chicken alive and kicking for a little while longer, the growth spurt driven by Dave's cowboys was a significant feature of DHL's emergence, but not a rock-solid base upon which to build a sustainable global business and culture.

But Not Sustainable

By 1979, DHL's "arrival" was precarious and something had to be done. As Po Chung says:

> Though we had grown from local to global quite organically, without a global headquarters to provide centralized decision-making, this sort of behavior wasn't suited for scaling up to create a complex, multinational system. We prided ourselves on our diffuse, local knowledge, but we didn't have the structures in place to become an effective global organization. This is where we needed management, consolidation, and structure.

So the problem wasn't thinking or acting locally, a problem of adaptation which bedeviled most multinationals leaving home to conquer the world; no, DHL's problem was the converse, how to act and think and organize globally.

In 1979, the founders hired Bill Walden as the company's first global CEO. Bill was an experienced executive who had made his name successfully turning around a federation of Australian insurance companies, building a successful national network out of a group of disparate entities. Not quite the blueprint for DHL, but the ingredients were clearly there. Bill had a look at what DHL had achieved, and came to a typically laconic conclusion: "it's a bit of a mess, but it has money."[2]

Bill Walden

---

2 As recalled by Roger Bowie.

Bill was given a free mandate, with the one proviso that the young men and women who had thus far given DHL such a spectacular start be given a chance to grow up along with the company. Bill was in his sixties, and the young DHL managers he found around the world were on average half his age. To them he was an old man. And so he became "the old man," an affectionate if somewhat apprehensive reflection of the respect which Bill quickly earned, albeit tinged with the fear and uncertainty which change brings. The term of course implies patriarch, and this he also became, as a father figure and mentor to many of the young managers that he found getting in each other's way as they strived to move up whatever ladder appeared before them.

Structure to Support a Growth Strategy

After establishing a small team in Hong Kong and taking stock of what the immediate cash position was, and the immediate issues requiring attention, he started to build structure, but not at the center. It was intuitive anathema to the DHL founders to create a large head office, in keeping with the decentralized, bottom-up approach which had clearly worked to get the business to where it was. Po Chung spent 18 months with Bill as he spent time in Hong Kong, London and San Francisco. It was partly an induction process for Bill, but also a learning experience for Po, as between them they worked on what needed to be done to sustain the business without sacrificing those soft assets which were clearly working. Larry, of course, was also involved, and Dave soon after became President of DHL USA.

A decentralized approach was clearly working, so, the structure was not to be command and control, but to be regional, in keeping with an emerging philosophy to empower decision making as close to the customer as possible. And while there was little precedent on how to organize globally, perhaps only in the banking sector, the first cut was, on the surface, surprising. Fifteen regions took shape, two in Asia, two in Europe, two in Africa, four within the US, and then the Middle East, Latin (South) America, and three large "country" regions, UK & Ireland, Canada and shortly thereafter, Mexico. A combination of strategy, size and pragmatism, the latter specifically aligned to the quality of people available or in place. Strategically, the USA was important as the economic powerhouse of the world, so a decentralized focus within the U.S. was deemed to be required to accelerate growth. Africa was a geographical and political challenge, with South Africa seen as a pariah state elsewhere on the continent. South America was just getting started, and Mexico and Canada just didn't fit with the USA folk and their relative inexperience of working outside their home environment. The UK was the second largest individual market, and Europe was still underdone with a presence mainly in the capital cities. For the most part, these regions were to be managed by young managers already available to move or already in place. But beefed up by an influx of more professional managers to fill the gap in what was for the most part an operational group, people who had started as couriers worked their way up in the frenzy of late 70s expansion. So, in came the finance managers, the sales and marketing managers, and increasingly a team of data people at the forefront of the information technology age just taking shape.

At a corporate level, a tax-effective corporate ownership structure was embedded, and a management consultancy company set up to house the global management team. The unimaginatively named Management Resources International (MRI) was moved to London as a low-key, low-profile head office that was not a head office, but a service company, providing services to the regions. There was of course a tax advantage in not having a branded and owned headquarters, which complemented the neatness of the Dutch arrangements whereby the countries were owned by one group, and the network by a subsidiary of DHL International Hong Kong. Was DHL American, Chinese, Dutch or British? Answer: none of the above. That's how it looked, and that was how it felt to the fifteen regional managers. In theory, the management services offered by MRI were contestable, but no one had the inclination or courage to dispense with the old man's services! Besides, everyone was having too much fun, because the singular focus was growth, but this time within a modicum of structure and process, and the occasional grumpy outburst (from Bill).

With a New Confidence

By 1981, DHL was organized and ready to tell the world. The suspension of the UK postal monopoly had given the company a much-needed boost of confidence, and the marketing campaign started the day after with a television advertisement depicting the DHL paper plane whooshing round the world like a paper dart, with the tagline "you couldn't express it better." A few years earlier, consensus had been reached on the use of a logo, and now that logo was being flashed proudly as the symbol of an emerging brand. Managers now noticed a shift in market perception and knowledge. For most of the 70s an answer to the question "who do you work for?" required a lengthy explanation of what it was that DHL did, and with the challenges of language this explanation required some effort. Korean businessmen were very impressed to see that the document just delivered had been handled by a "Korea service"; on the other hand, explaining the service in French was fraught with risk, as the word *courrier* in the French language was the generic term for "mail." So it came as a source of much pride, and occasional relief, to discover that more questions could be answered simply by saying "DHL," and people would recognize the name and the service.

DHL had started advertising in the U.S., but the "paper plane" ad signaled the one area of business where the center would take an overt lead, creating and coordinating a worldwide advertising campaign, mainly in print media, but also television in countries where the regulatory regimes had relaxed to the extent that undue publicity would not be a negative phenomenon.

Coming Out

Thus it was in Athens, in late 1981, that Bill Walden and his MRI team brought the fifteen regions together for the first global business meeting in DHL's now twelve-year history. Delegates were greeted on arrival with a mocked-up edition of that day's International Herald Tribune with the front page dedicated to DHL's first global conference, which was described as "high-level discussions on global strategy which will lead to substantially greater efficiency and coordination." Larry was there, but didn't appear in the photo.

The DHL network represented at the 1981 conference comprised 263 "stations," or cities, in 65 countries, up from 18 US offices and 23 international cities in 1974, with a worldwide employee base of 4,400, and turnover between $300 and $400 million. Every seven minutes a plane would take off somewhere within this vast network with a DHL courier on board, along the way providing a much needed financial contribution to the global airline industry. A spokesman proudly confirmed through the mock-up that DHL's success was due to the fact that it was not a multinational, with strong central control, but a network where the regions operated with a high level of autonomy, with the exception being overall financial planning and advertising, to complement the various local and regional budgets. The regional managers spoke of innovations occurring in their territories, along with a show and tell of their businesses' vital statistics. Interestingly, the meeting was peppered with representatives and examples of early diversification, which largely reflected Larry's obsession with technology and its threat to the core business of physical document delivery. The Business Systems division was there, talking about the early efforts to build information systems which would also allow electronic transmission of documents which could be printed and delivered by the network. And a telex store-and-forward business was also present, which allowed for consolidation of telex messages into high speed bursts of transmission, not only creating economies of scale, but also leveraging lower rates in certain countries, such as the newly deregulated UK, an early example of global arbitrage.

The Athens meeting thus encapsulated the hallmarks of the Walden years: budgetary discipline and accountability, local autonomy supported by broader business and marketing skills, global coordination of a limited number of activities, carefully selected diversification to complement and protect the core business, and an unrelenting focus on the Peter Drucker mantra that the customer alone provides employment.

And Cash is the King

This annual meeting format became a key event for DHL and for the regional managers, who would make an annual trek to obscure parts of the world and present their achievements, their plans and budgets for the forthcoming year. Mazatlán, Guam, Barbados, Bermuda, Mombasa all featured as destinations which saw young managers arrive from all over the world, nervous about their presentations, apprehensive about their plans, in some cases wondering if their job would be different by the end of the week, and occasionally whether they had a job at all. But they also came to have fun, and to share experiences with their colleagues, whom for the most part they would only see once a year at this meeting. Friendships were made, barriers broken down and problems solved as everyone recognized and understood the others' challenges, and the fact that they were for the most part the same issues all over the world. The small MRI finance team worked feverishly during the week of the meeting to compile a consolidated view for Bill and his team, such that the growing list of capital projects could be prioritized and approved. For several years running, the demand on cashflow was so great, that regions would be asked to go back and present revised plans, which committed to generating more cash for an increasingly capital hungry business. Aggressive growth in terms of continued geographical expansion, was also being met by increasing demand from the existing network, and an increasing requirement for infrastructure to support the growing number of packages to be sorted in the local warehouses as well as international transfer hubs.

Thus, Bill Walden structured and then steered this "mess with money" through a critical period in its history, where rapid growth, ongoing regulatory pressure, the threat of new and powerful international competition would have imperiled the business had it stayed organized as it was in 1979. And along the way, made some of the biggest business decisions not only of his own business life, but certainly for the survival or otherwise of DHL as an emerging global brand and as a private entity.

After four years of the fifteen-region structure, another organizational effort reconstructed the regions into more logical geographical and market groupings. Europe became one region, in line with the growing importance of building a European overnight service capability to mirror the FedEx model in the USA, and also pre-empt their heralded entry into the global arena. Similarly, the USA collapsed into one unit, as they also took on the domestic giants, FedEx and UPS, in providing overnight domestic services within the US, another effort to delay if not prevent their international plans. Africa also became one region, and then Bill appointed two deputies, splitting the world into two, the Americas and the Rest of the World. Thus the 1985 conference in Kenya saw a slimmed-down conference, and evidence of succession planning as Bill approached retirement.

The following year he did indeed retire, and then sadly passed away a few months later. But the seven or so years of his tenure left DHL vastly different, and considerably matured.

Chapter 12
Business Innovation

In the 70s DHL defined, designed and implemented the core processes which characterize the courier systems of today. Door-to-door, onboard couriers, progressive consolidation, simple all-inclusive pricing and total control, supported by low- and no-tech systems such as color-coded bags and physical exchange of proofs of delivery were the hallmarks of the first decade. A willingness to respond to customer requirements heralded the fundamentals of business which were written into management textbooks in the 80s and 90s. The Walden and early Lupo years also saw much innovation, within the context of greater structure and discipline which was a prerequisite to sustain the early success of a business of DHL's size.

Getting it There in No Time at All

In the early 70s, the banking industry was quick to understand the value of speed and the impact of DHL's door-to-door service on their ability to offer, in turn, a rapid clearance facility for foreign currency checks. Despite the prediction from Citibank in 1960 that banking transactions would be paperless by 1980, the check was still the predominant way in which people and businesses exchanged money for payment or reward. While the letter of credit unlocked the fulfillment supply chain, the check completed it, and business was frustrated by the length of time it took for checks to be cleared. Not surprisingly, DHL played a major role in speeding up both processes, the dispatch of the original letter of credit, and the collection of foreign currency checks for clearance in their country of currency. The U.S. dollar was by far the largest currency of international trade, and so U.S. checks could be found anywhere in the world, of only promissory value until finally cleared by the Reserve Bank Clearing House in New York, a process which could take weeks. Working closely with Bankers Trust (who set up DHL collection processes worldwide, and made a side business from offering earlier access to cleared funds) and other big banks, one solution was to put a courier on Concorde every day between London and New York. Specifically targeted at London's financial district, collections could be made as late as 3:30 p.m., and scrambled to Heathrow Airport for the 5:30 pm Concorde. 5:30 p.m. is 12:30 p.m. New York (Eastern Standard) time, and with ascent, lunch on board, and descent, DHL's courier arrived in New York at approximately 4:00 p.m. local time (Concorde's flight time to New York being approximately 3.5 hours). Cut off time at New York's

https://doi.org/10.1515/9781501507557-015

clearing house was 5:00 p.m., so the only way to beat the traffic was by helicopter, a ten-minute journey from John F. Kennedy airport into the World Trade Center in Manhattan. The fastest possible journey between the City of London and Manhattan was enjoyed by many an amazed DHL courier, and millions of dollars were made by the clearing banks through faster access to funds. Ultimately, of course, the wheels of commerce turned ever faster as a result of this innovative service.

Tentative Steps to Expand the Offering

One of the major contributing factors to early success and such rapid growth was the fact that only business documents of no commercial value were carried. Given all the barriers which existing regulation threw at the fledgling global, this was a necessary and astute focus on the core, and undoubtedly the relative ease of customs clearance procedures for non-dutiable items, be it on the freight side or in the baggage halls, helped build a system which consistently delivered speed of transit from door-to-door. With the exception of a side venture flying perishables throughout the islands of Hawaii, DHL stuck to its knitting for most of the 70s, and was kept frantically busy dealing with increased customer demand and network expansion.

Toward the end of this decade, however, the opportunity to expand the product offering to include small items with a commercial value, became evident, both from customer requests as well as witnessing the fate of small items within the airfreight process, which concentrated on the big stuff. The ongoing threat of retaliatory action from the postal authorities, along with the perceived threat of substitution from emerging data transmission technologies also drove DHL to look to the small parcel market to protect its future.

Early efforts in this regard had focused on getting spare parts into the Middle East, and particularly into Saudi Arabia, driven by demand from the big oil companies and their supporting services and construction businesses providing infrastructure and peripheral services to the unquenchable thirst for more oil. But the process of getting goods into Saudi Arabia was vastly different from simply moving documents. Every commercial invoice had to be translated into Arabic and pre-authorized by Saudi consular officials seeking to ensure their trade embargo against Israel was not being breached by goods manufactured by companies on their "blacklist." And that was before the complex customs clearance process. DHL mitigated the challenges by airfreighting the goods into Bahrain, where airside access was available, taking care of the consularization process in down-town Manama, and then using an onboard courier (who spoke Arabic) to fly di-rectly into Riyadh, taking the daily chance with passenger customs.

This hybrid process was both innovative and pragmatic, and typical of DHL to hone its early experience in the most challenging of environments, but the core challenges were laid bare. Moving items with a commercial value meant that cus-toms regulations and tariffs had to be understood in every country. There was no single source for all this knowledge, which is understandably why the customs brokerage industry had grown worldwide to dominate the import process. And where there did exist a knowledge source (e.g. a book of import tariffs) it didn't necessary follow that the rules would be applied consistently, especially in devel-oping countries. This was a huge challenge, and one which would take more than a decade of persistence before it could be said that DHL was truly in the express freight business. And so in the 80s it was a case of trial and error, and a process of identifying segments which were easier to clear through customs, particularly in the baggage halls. So the package business slowly grew as a series of lists, country by country, of goods and value thresholds eligible for the Small Package Express (SPX) service as it came to be known and marketed. Samples, not for resale, were an easy target, as were items which stretched the imagination to be described as documents, such as computer tapes, and media artwork. But the limitations to the service, and the changing conditions of eligibility (the "list" often had to be re-vised based on practical experience, based on customs whims, and not always based on any clear logic) was frustrating to both customers and DHL personnel alike. The small package service, later renamed as WPX (Worldwide Package Ex-press), grew in fits and starts, not in tidal waves of demand as had been the case with the document service. Green bags were now complemented by red bags for the dutiable items, and it was often the case that green was for go, and red was for stop, in terms of the speed and reliability of the service.

The introduction of the SPX/WPX service did force a change in the way data was captured, however, and this proved to be critical in the near future as cus-toms increasingly required information in advance as a prerequisite to providing a fast clearance process to match that in place for documents. Up until then, man-ifesting was simply a matter of recording the consignee which sufficed to match shipments on arrival and capture billing data for the few customers who had cen-tralized billing. But for dutiable items, customs required full consignee as well as content description, and if these data were available in advance, DHL could pre-pare all clearance paperwork, and submit when the goods had arrived. This pro-cess gradually became fully automated as customs systems improved. Advanced capture and transmission of data also served the growing requirement to offer a positive tracking system, as well as a tracing system for proof of delivery. Transitioning to an express parcel capability was a mountain to be climbed, one step at a time.

If You Can Get to the Internationally Remote Places, Why Not Just Down the Road?

DHL's chosen market position was to deliver internationally, and then globally. Federal Express on the other hand, chose its "knitting" to be within the United States, and by 1980 they had built a phenomenally successful domestic business guaranteeing overnight delivery between any two major cities within the USA. In doing so, they stayed largely under the regulatory radar, instead tackling the more capital-intensive struggle to justify dedicated air capacity on every route while volumes built. And when they did come under the scrutiny of the postal authorities, they argued for exemption based on an overnight or twelve-hour rule of delivery time, which left DHL exposed on its own to defend its international business. Consequently, the two companies were not the best of friends, and DHL watched warily for signs of a FedEx move beyond the U.S. borders. Management in the U.S. were also keen to take FedEx on in their own backyard: customers were wanting DHL to service their domestic needs, not understanding the logic of not being offered, for example, a Houston to New York service, when both cities were being served for international traffic. Moreover, management argued, if DHL takes on FedEx (and United Parcel Service for that matter) in their home market, they will be delayed if not diverted from seeking to go international.

And so in 1983 the momentous decision was made to launch a domestic service within the United States, with the attendant capital costs of ensuring dedicated aircraft flew every night, regardless of volume. Instead of mimicking FedEx with their single hub in Memphis, DHL decided to operate two hubs, one in Salt Lake City, the other in Cincinnati, a decision driven by the need to minimize the step-cost effect by using smaller aircraft, which would not have the capacity/speed combination to fly to a single point and back again. Later on, as volume grew, the two-hub system was reduced to a single hub in Cincinnati. The objective was to capture ten percent of the domestic market, a threshold deemed sufficient to keep an even keel with FedEx and UPS as they eyed up the international market.

Europe Overnight

While the decision to invest in a domestic service within the U.S. was, to quote Bill Walden, "the biggest business decision DHL will ever make," doing the same thing within "the United States of Europe" was a more natural evolution of the core business. After all, there were still customs clearance between all European countries, and road transport could offer an effective, and much cheaper, over-night service between many European cities (this was the domain where TNT and IPEC, the Australian firms, placed their bets). But the option of Europe overnight, anywhere to anywhere, was still open, and in the early 80s, DHL stepped up to this challenge using Frankfurt as the hub. By 1982, DHL employed sixty staff at Frankfurt Airport, receiving the inbound material from Austria, Italy, Greece, London and New York accompanied by on-board couriers, and from Switzerland, Belgium, Holland and all major German cities by road. Finally, material from Scandinavia and France would arrive on light aircraft owned and operated by a DHL subsidiary for these routes. Material would be broken down, sorted, and re-consolidated in the space of three hours, from midnight to 3:00 a.m., before the outbound service started. In this way, DHL could offer close of business pickup and before noon delivery between all major cities in Europe.

In 1985, more favorable conditions (ground space, rentals, and most im-portantly the ability to fly in and out at night) were offered at Zaventem airport in Brussels, and the hub moved there just in time to be able to cope with the in-creased volume and the larger aircraft required to maintain the service. Mechani-zation appeared, in the form of an initially underwhelming single line conveyor system which enabled easier handling of the large volumes of green and (occa-sional) red bags, and so DHL entered the era where industrial engineering, as a business skill, was necessary to replace the seat-of-the-pants frenzy which typi-fied the explosive growth of the 70s. To be fair, the mechanized sorting facilities in Cincinnati were much more high-tech and futuristic given the size of the do-mestic market within the US.

As in the U.S., providing overnight service from a central hub inevitably re-quired dedicated aircraft, because commercial carriers, not surprisingly, did not fly without passengers, who in turn did not want to fly during the night. DHL in Europe needed to partner with or acquire local airlines who were providing over-night cargo services and who had the requisite flying and landing rights. This development, along with the mechanization, provided capacity for growth, and the demand from customers was clearly there. At last, the WPX service took off. Numbers of packages processed through the Brussels hub compared to numbers of documents told the story. In August 1985 daily WPX volumes (by weight, not numbers) were 21 percent of document volumes. By December 1987 there was equivalence! WPX volumes had grown by nearly 800 percent, while document volumes grew by 64 percent. Twenty tons of documents, and twenty tons of WPX were being processed every night.[1]

And What About a Second Brand?

In the same spirit of diversification and pre-emption which drove the decision to invest in a U.S. domestic service, DHL looked at the UK and European markets with their well-developed but highly fragmented intra and inter-country trucking services. There was both opportunity in developing critical mass from which to grow further through acquisition, as well as putting a stick in the spokes of their emerging global competitor TNT, which was expanding its express services by acquiring IPEC/Skypak to complement their European overnight road services. In 1981, DHL UK had acquired a small airfreight company (initially to support the growth of the parcel business) as well as a domestic courier business which had proven to be a successful partner in servicing the cities outside of London. With these businesses as a base, the operation was renamed DHL Elan, which set about building domestic long-haul services within the UK and Germany (where UPS had its only international presence with a three–four day service trucking operation).

Early Computerization

As we have seen, Larry was an early adopter of technologies, partly because he could see the future impact as an opportunity, partly as a threat, as electronic data transmission cannibalized the physical document. The initial focus was on word processing, to support administrative processes, but also as a platform to ultimately engage in moving documents as data between offices throughout the world, effectively disintermediating the airline as the carrier. And the fax machine, which was now a commercial reality, was seen as the first major step in this process of substitution. At the same time that large scale efforts were being made, particularly in the Middle East, to reinvent DHL effectively as a technology company, some managers, ignoring the hype, turned their attention to how technology could help with the core business, which was still dependent on manual and physical processes such as manifesting, proof of delivery, and billing.

---

1 Source: Stephen Fenwick (DHL employee 1976–2016) historical records.

When Bill Walden did his situation analysis, he found a smattering of local initiatives looking at data processing, all well-meaning, but not connected or co-ordinated into the vision he was beginning to project as he brought structure in. For example, in Bahrain talks were at an advanced stage to outsource the billing processes to a third-party bureau. That initiative clearly wasn't scalable, so it was put on hold and Bill hired an IT guy from IBM, who focused on the business process issues as opposed to the product opportunities which Larry was promoting and which were led by a more academic group based in Washington and Silicon Valley. Around this time, IBM started releasing its range of mini or mid-range computing systems starting with the IBM 34, and in 1983 the IBM 36, which became the workhorse for DHL for the foreseeable future, providing support for back office processes such as accounting and billing, and operational systems such as manifesting.

These of course were small and laborious early steps, as computers were new and foreign to most of DHL's young, operations-oriented workforce. Capturing data from the proliferation of paper-based forms was the early focus, and the IBM 36 environment offered tantalizing opportunity to turn data into information because of its enhanced report-writing capability. But management didn't really know what reports they wanted, and the default position of a computer-illiterate management team was to say to the techies, "you make it up, and we'll tell you if it's what we want." There was both a lack of knowledge and methodology when it came to identifying business requirements before the system or software was designed and deployed. So for most of the decade, the solution was to use the System 36 query function, and to train management to ask computer-coded questions of their increasingly rich database.

Data capture was the key to unlocking the fruits of computerization, and the input of manifesting records (initially to trigger billing) was in due course complemented by entry of delivery information, and began the process of reducing, then ultimately eliminating the labor-intensive process of returning the physical POD. The use of the fax machine which took off in the early 80s with the release of several commercial brands of lightweight fax machines also supported the process of automating the tracking process. But more influential was the arrival of barcoding technology to a level of economic viability, and in the mid-80s DHL produced its first barcoded airway bills and began to process auto-captured shipment numbers.

What Aided and Abetted Also Threatened

From inception, Larry understood that technology was going to be a key factor in gaining and maintaining a market-leading position in its chosen niche. However, the same technologies which improved the global exchange of data and images also threatened to substitute for the physical mode of transmitting information via a document. Hence the early efforts to enter the word processing market through DHL Systems and its DHL 1000 word processor, an effort which gained some foothold in the Middle East in the late 70s and early 80s, due to its Arabic language capability, but hardly the platform for global domination. First Wang and then the PC took care of that.

In the early 80s, Larry's focus turned to newer technologies which were disrupting the current breed of computer processing and adding exciting new possibilities for data transmission between machines wherever in the world they might be. Distributed computing was becoming a viable option, made possible by new operating systems such as Unix, and with that the idea of a hybrid offering combining digital transmission of documents, via computer or fax machine, with high quality printing and physical delivery. The idea was to combine the pick-up and delivery of a physical document, and substitute the air carrier with an electronic transmission to enable overnight delivery virtually anywhere. Anywhere, that is, with a suitable fax machine and access to suitable telecommunications services which provided for reliable, fast transmission of data.

Of course, at that time, fax and telecommunications were both unreliable and limited in geographic penetration. For a start, faxes were perishable, with poor printing quality which deteriorated in a few short weeks, if not altogether faded away. And the international telephone services into many developing countries were abominably poor. For example, getting a call through to Lagos, Nigeria, from Tunis, Tunisia often involved a two-week wait for an operator-assisted service. Messaging via DHL internal mail was much more efficient and reliable.

So, there were no magical solutions to protecting DHL's position through an electronic equivalent; but Larry was ahead of his time in envisaging what was to become a reality starting some ten years later with the commercialization of the internet. And Larry no longer needed nor wanted to be involved in the day-to-day management of DHL, which had been entrusted to Bill Walden. So DHL Systems in San Francisco, and its sister company Net Express out of Washington, D.C., explored high -speed data transmission strategies (using the newly invented x.25 packet switching protocols) combined with Group 4 fax technologies (which provided for lossless quality transmission and printing) to enter the disruptive new world of telecommunications, opening up as a consequence of the deregulation and accompanying break-up of the old telecom monopolies. The vision for DHL was to station several of these high-cost, high-resolution fax machines in major cities well-serviced by fast telecom infrastructure, and offer a hybrid service, thereby allowing customers to access the new technologies with minimal capital outlay. Satellite Express was born, with overnight and same-day service capability.

But Also Provided Opportunity

Another investment in a technology/telecommunications business brought more immediate benefit in terms of both revenues (from customers) and costs savings to DHL. This occurred with the dual acquisition of Comswitch and Lydiastar. Both businesses offered "store-and-forward" telex services, using the store-and-forward protocols used by the earliest form of the internet, whereby messages, in this case telex messages, were consolidated at a country exit point, batch-processed over high speed lines to another country, reconsolidated, deconsolidated and finally sent to the recipient. A mirror image of how the courier service obtained economies of scale and leveraged lower costs from the airlines; in this case, the newly deregulated UK telecommunications market had allowed for a breaking of the monopoly price umbrella, and thus it was cheaper to send a telex from, say America to France, by switching the message via the UK. Processing was possible in the few hours when both continents were asleep, and so an early arbitrage service was possible with no perception of loss of immediacy by sender or receiver. The product lifecycle was short, however, and the service hung on by switching faxes as the use of the telex machine declined, only to be put to pasture by the arrival of the internet in the early 90s. The store-and-forward technique, however, survived technological substitution to be the predominant way in which billing and tracking data was shared across DHL regions using dedicated, leased lines connecting up the network of IBM 36s.

Building a Brand

In the previous chapter, we mentioned introduction of centrally coordinated advertising which signaled the arrival of Bill Walden's global management team, the first gathering of DHL managers from all over the world, and the hugely morale boosting suspension of the postal monopoly which occurred in the United Kingdom. The choice of advertising as one of the few activities which DHL would control from the center, in contrast to its clear philosophy of decentralized management in virtually all other management areas, was deliberate and calculated. Building a global brand was not for the faint-hearted, particularly when greater awareness might yet backfire into regulatory retaliation; nor were the benefits always understood by a network of local managers, each with their own budgets and market sensitivities to be catered to, be aware and beware of. But DHL leaders clearly saw the advantages of a common image, a common look and feel, and a common set of messages to underpin what was becoming a key point of difference: DHL in control, from door-to-door, from go to whoa!

Hence along with the advertising came a refresh of the logo and global standards for vehicle signage, uniforms and customer packaging (the DHL Flyer was a strengthened polyethylene envelope designed to contain and protect up to 1kg of documents). Putting signage on the vehicles was a low-cost way to spread the word, but a slow-mover. Global advertising provided a quantum leap in recognition, but was expensive and therefore sporadic. Last, but not least, there were branding guidelines and specifications for how the logo, tagline and company name were to be projected on all media. As managers began to feel the early impact of brand awareness through not having to explain what DHL did when asked who they worked for, having a consistent image and message reinforced that trend. Thus began the creation of a very rare brand story–the building of a global brand name with little or no obvious connection to the activity undertaken (unless you were a competitor denigrating the origins of the founders' initials).

Ongoing Geographical Expansion

While the Walden years were characterized by building structure, bringing in new skill sets, and maturing the substantial global footprint established by the end of the 70s, there were still new frontiers to cross. The huge investments made in sustaining a market position in the USA and Europe, were complemented by rapid expansion into the developing world. Despite the perceived threat of substitution by technology, growth in the core business was assured by the pace of new entrants into the network, at a rate of approximately one new city every eight days.

First, Latin America and the Caribbean took off. In 1982 alone, twenty-four countries in South and Central America including the Caribbean were added to the network. Yes, some of these were very small island territories, but it all added up to the growing realization within DHL that the network was the major asset, and DHL's geographical mission was quite simply, to be everywhere.

In 1980, only five countries in Africa were being serviced (South Africa, Zimbabwe, Kenya, Ivory Coast and Nigeria). By 1988 over fifty countries were open for business. And in 1983 the first DHL tentacles spread cautiously into the Eastern bloc countries, in many cases building agency relationships with local state providers as a first step towards incorporating independently in later years when circumstances allowed. Service to Russia commenced in 1984 and in 1986 an agreement was signed with Sinotrans, the large state-owned domestic transport conglomerate in the People's Republic of China. Much of the early efforts into the Communist bloc countries were led by Dave Allen, still searching for new territories to conquer! Dave's unbridled optimism and passion were contagious, even in the most challenging environments, underpinned by patience and persistence in the face of obstacles and negotiating tactics which would have seen many others give up. By the end of the decade there were few countries left; until of course the collapse of the Soviet Union created a dozen or so more!

The DHL logo was consistently displayed on all forms of transport, and the vehicles used for conveyance were across the spectrum. It was a long way from the nondescript and often battered range of second-hand cars used by the early pioneer couriers in London. The Boeing 727 was the workhorse in the air, complemented by a range of smaller jet and propeller aircraft, particularly the Fokker F27 and the Convair 580. Then on the ground, DHL couriers would use vans, cars, motorcycles and increasingly heavy trucks on long sectors which could be served overnight by road. Boats were also used, in places like Venice and Amsterdam, as well as buses which could also serve as mobile sorting centers, such as in Hong Kong and Dublin. The principle of allowing management freedom to act and to innovate as close to the customer as possible, and only at a later stage imposing a common identity on all this variation, was a key factor in the rapid growth, constant innovation and inexorable geographical expansion which occurred during the 80s.

Less than Door-to-door

As DHL in the USA and then Europe began to deploy dedicated aircraft on certain sectors, principally to support the domestic and Europe overnight service, spare capacity and sector imbalances became an issue. To maintain a consistent service, the aircraft had to fly regardless of load. Monday was always a heavy inbound day, but light on the outbound. Tuesday was always slower than Friday. Airline economics dictate that the aircraft must always be used, but that a minimum load factor must be consistently met before break even. New products were needed to fill the spare capacity. And "filler freight" was also required. In the U.S., one answer was to launch a general freight service to anywhere in the world, door to airport, using the domestic capacity to collect the freight, fly it to an export gateway, when a commercial carrier would be used, and then get it to the destination airport, where the receiving customer would be expected to clear and collect the consignment. While this effort helped the U.S. defray the costs of the dedicated air capacity servicing the domestic network, both DHL and customers at the international destinations were often confused about the status of such shipments and where the responsibility lay for final delivery.

In Europe, the approach was more disciplined and clear-cut. Within Europe, and between Europe and the U.S., once DHL freighters began flying that route, the service was confined to airport-to-airport consignments. The perceived problem was that the best paying customers for this type of service were often competitors. European managers were up in arms about the threat of undermining their own business by letting competing material fly on DHL aircraft. The response was that without the revenue from that traffic, costs would go up, and price competitiveness would be threatened. Seemed like a Catch-22, but in reality, the country managers were forgetting about the power of the last ten yards. If you owned the total door-to-door, desk-to -desk service, there was always a subtle but important competitive advantage to be maintained. And so it turned out that the General Freight Service, or GFS, became an integral part of the dedicated air component of DHL's service.

Early Steps in Logistics

Toward the end of the decade, considerable physical capacity had been acquired at airports which functioned as transfer points or hubs. At the same time, many technology companies were extending their product range into services such as repair and return or replace. Modern production techniques with lower component costs meant that the costs of distribution now became a much more significant cost in the entire supply chain, particularly if those lower costs components were being made or assembled in different countries around the globe. And with more streamlined manufacturing techniques, replacement of faulty parts became more economical than repair. Whether a business model involved repair or replacement, it made sense for the spare parts to be housed close to the customer for reasons of both cost and speed of response. DHL's hubs made ideal warehouses for the storage of these spare parts, and so the concept of Express Logistics or Parts Centers took shape.

In Singapore, Hewlett Packard created significant competitive advantage by storing computer parts in a DHL warehouse close to Changi airport and offering its many distributors throughout Southeast Asia a free replacement service for any PC or component deemed faulty. No questions asked. DHL's long and arduous journey from being simply a courier of documents to becoming an integrated logistics business was starting to bear fruit.

Answer the Phone, Dammit!

One of the things which Bill Walden emphasized when he joined DHL in 1979 was the power of the telephone and the call center as an extension of the sales force. As a result of a decade of deregulation in the telecommunications industry the costs of communicating dropped considerably and call centers for sales and customer service were now a standard part of any company's toolkit. The problem then became how to maintain a quality service at the end of the line as call volumes and customer expectations grew. Waiting for the phone to be answered was not at that point in time the issue it was to become twenty years later as companies tried to get people off the phones and onto a website for their customer service, but it was still an issue. And in a competitive environment where express companies were experimenting with service level guarantees, DHL had to step up in areas where it exercised sufficient control. The common ground became the time taken to answer the phone, made possible and measurable by new call monitoring technology. And so, at first in Asia, then elsewhere, the guarantee was to answer the phone within three rings or the shipment went free!

Chapter 13
Business Context—What Was Going on Here?

A New Era of Globalization Begins

The 1980s heralded a thirty-year global transformation based on the power of the market, an indefatigable belief in the ability of increasingly unfettered commerce and free trade to be a fundamental platform for economic growth and prosperity. This is or was a belief which is now being challenged by, on the one hand, disgruntled voters in Europe, the United Kingdom and the U.S. questioning the benefits of globalization. And on the other hand, the continued success of the Asian economies, where the model has been one of more direct government intervention and direction. But in those heady days, the markets ruled, and certainly the globalization of commerce was seen for the most part as a force for good, as consumer power and ability to consume was shared by all.

The growth of Japan and the Asian tigers (Korea, Taiwan, Hong Kong, Singapore) showed three things: first that the sourcing, production and distribution of products can occur without the constraints of national borders; second, that companies can globalize from anywhere, not just America and Europe; third, the role of government in encouraging instead of regulating commerce can have a dramatic effect on economic growth and prosperity, echoing Larry's early views some ten years previously.

What this meant was that the great manufacturing businesses in the U.S., UK and Europe could see a tantalizingly steep decline in their cost curves, by taking advantage of the permissive environments in Asia, where foreign direct investment was encouraged, and production could be shifted to business-friendly environments with eager workforces available to work at a lower cost. Deregulation as a philosophy was espoused by the UK and U.S. governments with Europe being forced to follow, with a European Treaty, albeit until now dormant, in place to provide momentum. Deregulation also anticipated or followed fast behind advances in technology which disrupted transportation and communications to make the world a more connected place. This time was different from the great global movement of the previous century in that everyone could now play. And, buoyed by quickly reduced costs of transportation and communications it was actually companies which traded, not countries. Trade policy however, was still more restrictive than facilitative, as vested lobby interests in several countries in several sectors resisted the potential loss of the protected access to domestic markets which had been the norm until now.

https://doi.org/10.1515/9781501507557-016

DHL provided a solution to the problem of conducting business on a global scale by providing a channel through which essential business information, in hard copy, could be shared or distributed globally. A channel fast enough to recognize and preserve the intangible value of time being of the essence. Such connectivity allowed for better integration of activities between separate countries, thus enabling the speeding-up of the processes of sourcing, production and distribution—a forerunner of the fully integrated supply chain models which emerged in later decades. This was the beginning of the era of "speed to market" as a defining characteristic of who would win the competitive battle. It was also when Japanese companies were producing high quality, lower cost product by employing "just-in-time" methods. Being able to operate with less inventory and smaller factories added another dimension to bending the cost curve using techniques other than low-cost labor. Within companies, the notion of "logistics" was being explored, initially as a coordinating role between the demand and supply aspects of the business, as opposed to the control factor which the logistics discipline later exerted on supply chain management.

In fact, with the exception of those Japanese manufacturers, companies still saw the process of sourcing, production and distribution as three sub-systems of their overall enterprise, and while the 80s saw some moves to better coordinate, if not integrate the supply and demand sub-systems, production for the most part stayed in a world of its own[1]. That didn't matter; there was enough to do in just coordinating this huge surge in global activity, and for many, DHL's fast and reliable service became an essential component of the suite of services necessary to compete.

And by the end of the decade, high-tech companies were beginning to leverage the capability and capacity of DHL and other express companies to distribute from warehouses located close to or within the airport hubs. The notion of manufacturing simply being sourcing, production and distribution was changing to add service as an essential component, as the vendors offered value-added services dealing with repair, return or replacement of component parts. Even the manufacturing sector was embracing the age of the service sector and service mind set, helped by the ability to distribute information via the internet, and small commercial items via the express companies.

---

[1] John Gattorna, *Dynamic Supply Chains*, 3rd Edition, Pearson Education 2015, p. 16.

What was DHL Carrying?

At the height of the major postal battles throughout the 80s, DHL was able to mount a credible defense against the charge that it was carrying letters, as well as articulate what was essentially different about the service offered by traditional postal services. Some of these arguments were mirrored as some of the more recalcitrant defenders of the status quo squirmed their way into a regulatory compromise. At the top of most lists would be checks, drafts, promissory notes, letters of credit, bonds, other non-negotiable financial instruments, stock certificates, insurance policies; in short, all those paper based tools of trade of the financial industry. Then turn to the shipping industry, with manifests, bills of lading, insurance policies; construction companies would send plans, technical drawings, blueprints, and other detailed specifications designed to reduce the tyranny of distance which existed between the processes of design and build. Computer printouts were commonly sent by courier; in some cases, single consignments could stretch to over 1000 kilos in weight. And companies were now able to effectively participate in international tenders with more time for preparation, and the security of knowing the tender was signed for as proof of receipt. The list went on and on, to demonstrate that there was a huge distance between the definition of a letter being both current and personal and the actual usage by courier service customers. The service itself was clearly different from postal services, in that courier companies exercised control (security) over the service from door-to-door, were effectively able to guarantee delivery, provide proof of delivery, and offer a level of both consistency and reliability along with flexibility (for example to intervene during the document's transit to change its destination). Customers were baffled by the notion that a post office could prevent DHL from operating.

This Was an Outbound Phenomena

For the most part, however, this was an outbound service, in that it was originated by the sender, not the receiver. Certainly, this distinction is blurred when it comes to regular exchanges of pouches between multinationals on key routes, but what was more common in these types of exchanges was the fact that the service was for the most part originated by the company's head office, and the branches would follow. As mentioned above, this outbound orientation mirrored the lack of maturity we would later see with the integration of supply chains to, from and between different players engaged in the supply, production and distribution of a given product. Logistics was still a new term, as was supply chain management, and the first signs of integration started with coordination of sourcing with distribution, while production remained an island of independence. But even here, the predominant purchasing behavior was for someone to send something through DHL, rather than ask for it to be collected somewhere else and received. Suppliers were more frequently asked to send something via DHL and pay for it themselves, in order to satisfy their own customer's requirements.

In part, this was because DHL's systems were set up for outbound service, which made it easier to organize a homogenous service among a network of "independents" and kept things to the "KISS" principle (Keep It Simple, Stupid). But it was also because, in the traditional world of freight forwarding, the opposite was more the rule, in that the country of origin and the country of destination had separate roles to play, one for export and one for import. Customs regulations were focused on the fact that the principal party to a transaction was invariably based in the home country, and thus the processes for export relied on the declaration of the sender, while the processes of import relied heavily on the declarations of the receiver. Regulations were conceived in this way to maintain control of the passage of goods in and out of country. Hence the concept of controlling all of the international movements of goods, from sourcing of components to distribution of finished product, including the production or manufacturing process, was a long way from reality in the 80s. Logistics remained a fragmented discipline until the arrival of the internet which allowed for information flows to highlight the amount of inventory and where it was kept. This availability of better and faster information ultimately exposed the inefficiencies of an un-integrated system with its seeming inability to manage inventory and stock against surges in supply or demand. And by this stage, customs authorities were beginning to modernize their approach to accommodate the new economic realities.

Whether DHL influenced this reality, or simply responded to it is moot in the context of the challenges which it faced in entering the parcel or express freight market, and one of its biggest strengths, i.e. simplicity, became a future weakness in terms of lack of flexibility with any other than a prepaid term of trade. The billing processes which were automated in the early days of computerization were built around the core principle that the shipper paid, and the few significant exceptions to this rule (e.g. Bankers Trust organizing check collections from all around the world) were treated as such. Another exception existed from the outset, in that a number of U.S. corporations insisted on centralized billing (the rates from the U.S. were generally more favorable given the competitive situation) but even then, the workarounds were manual, and driven by two separate billing systems, one for the U.S., and a different system for the rest of the world.

The Information Age Beckoned, but Expensively

The impact of computer technologies along with faster and cheaper communications has been the principle driver of globalization and in the 80s business was seeing the opportunities as clearly as it was frustrating to realize the promise. While costs were coming down, technology and telecommunications were still expensive, and DHL in no small way compensated for this affordability gap with its fast, secure and reliable service for physical communication. But there was also a lack of experience with, as well as applications for the new technologies. Faster computing and faster movement of data were of little use if the core business processes were not encoded into applicable programs. DHL was an early adopter of technology, and, as already mentioned, a bleeding edge explorer of the boundaries of future potential. But the early efforts to automate understandably focused on the simple, outbound model which did not foresee the requirements for the more complex data capture requirements for customs clearance of dutiable items, nor the future customer demand for initiating an inbound shipment. This hardly mattered at the time, as the document business was growing at more than fifteen percent per annum, and the fax machine brought as much advantage if not more, than the threat of substitution. Fax was used for proof of delivery, advance dispatch of manifests, so destination countries knew what to expect (customs were also very keen to get this information) and from the customer's perspective, the faxing of documents was too expensive as a substitute for the courier. Also, the quality was poor, so that while a faxed signature might serve to keep the deal moving, it also increased the urgency for getting originals in place. The arrival of the fax arguably stimulated the growth of DHL's market, rather than hinder it. And let's not forget the costs of a fax machine, as well as a network of personal computers, was still a significant capital expenditure. A fax machine in Malawi cost $US 20,000 in 1986!

Airports Grew Up

In major airports such as London's Heathrow, Amsterdam's Schiphol, Hong Kong and Singapore's Changi, airlines created their own hub-and-spoke connections to link long-haul flights to local feeders. DHL naturally followed suit, and hence the prevalence of green bags clogging up the baggage carousels began to concern passengers, airlines and airport authorities alike. It wasn't uncommon for one courier to have fifty or sixty bags, and for some reason they all seemed to come out first, even ahead of the first-class baggage. The airlines were conflicted, as it was good business; the passengers most likely got over it, unless they were traveling every day, so the problem in the end became the airport's problem. DHL was sympathetic; the problem could be solved by providing fast clearance through the freight terminal, which would then save DHL lots of money by avoiding the costs of tickets and excess baggage. But, unless the service levels could be maintained, the couriers would keep flying in. After all, this was a business essential to doing business internationally, and most of the airlines' own commercial customers (for passenger and freight) relied on DHL's service.

From the perspective of customs, the "courier" issue had been manageable as long as the goods carried were just documents, with no commercial value, and no duties to collect. But because the customs and freight handling processes were designed around import and export as separate processes, with responsibility predominantly being taken by the local business involved (whether import or export) and with that responsibility being delegated to third-party brokers (customs clearance agents), DHL's fledgling parcel business was not given any special treatment through the freight channel. Moreover, DHL was not experienced at managing clearances of this nature, with the additional information which was required. So DHL sent its red bag service with its couriers and took its chances with customs in the baggage hall. Customs officers in the baggage halls were keen to get passengers and their baggage through as quickly as possible, but dealing with commercial goods in this way was not normal process.

Thus everyone began to have a problem with the courier-on-board phenomena, and this finally led to airport authorities and customs to work together for a better solution. It was not a straightforward issue; it was not a case of simply recreating the comparatively smooth process of clearing accompanied baggage on the freight side. If they did that for the couriers, why not do it for everybody? Why upset all the cozy relationships which have built up over the years and perpetuated the inefficiencies in process which arose from a culture of control, constraint and commission?

Not that easy. Too many vested interests, and those same vested interests also paid good rent to the airport authorities for their occupancy of another precious commodity, namely airport space. Real estate at busy airports is always scarce, so in addition to the prospect of upsetting existing tenants, the airport had to find extra room for the new service. Not surprisingly, therefore, it had to be treated as such, a new service, and not just for DHL, but for all the companies engaged in express courier or parcel services. By necessity, if not default, the airport authorities recognized a new industry, open to all players provided they pay the extra fees required to introduce the special handing processes required, and justify the creation of special facilities within which the activity could take place.

The same for customs. And so DHL started to win the battle of recognition that its service was new, vital, and valued, and the first breakthrough of this kind occurred at London's Heathrow, but the story was repeated over the years throughout the world. Heathrow built a dedicated facility for express handling and clearance, but the express companies had to pay a substantial premium for the privilege. The savings incurred through not buying tickets and paying excess baggage did not materialize to the extent that there was a huge drop in the price of the service. But it did pay for capacity to continue to grow, and that was most important to DHL. And with this came a new level of dialog with customs.

Strategic Disconnect

In the 80s, when DHL USA was focused on building volumes, both domestic and international, in order to fill belly-loads on expensive dedicated aircraft, U.S. outbound shipments grew faster than inbound. For the U.S. salesforce, price was always a function of a highly competitive market and the need to pre-empt the entry of FedEx and UPS into the international arena. It was, and then became, after the inevitable happened, a function of almost any price to achieve sales and volume growth.

For the rest of the world, however, the USA was just another country, just another sector among many, and price was not as sensitive from the international markets given DHL's dominant position, especially, for example, the strength of DHL service into the Middle East. International management were understandably reluctant to discount price on any sector if there was no competitive need to do so. And for the vast majority of international countries, airline costs were variable, as the commercial airlines continued to offer a reliable service on their passenger-based schedules.

As the decade unfolded, and the two U.S. giants made their move, this issue became somewhat of a strategic disconnect between the largest country in the network, albeit one of the least profitable, and the rest of the world, which was enjoying breakneck growth without having to compromise on yield. Thus, sector imbalances, which were not necessarily aligned to trade flows, became an Achilles heel in the effort to contain the spread of global competition. UPS and FedEx had no qualms about undercutting DHL pricing into the U.S., because they had both aircraft capacity to fill, as well as a domestic delivery cost advantage.

While this issue was understood intuitively by DHL global management, it was not objectively actionable in the absence of good data and analysis. This knowledge gap was initially filled through the extensive analysis done by the Bain teams in their strategic studies in the late eighties (see Chapter 18), but first, that knowledge took time to disseminate and be understood by DHL's predominantly operational cadre of management, and second, any strategic response to sector imbalances also required a greater knowledge of costs. DHL management were all too aware of the dangers of discounting without knowledge, given that cash was king, and the profitable markets and sectors, even if not enjoying optimal growth, were providing the oil to keep the global engine going.

The U.S. management exhorted their international colleagues to focus on America as a destination, even as a loss leader, to contain if not control FedEx and UPS. The USA was, after all, the economic powerhouse of the world! The rest of the world continued to grow exponentially across all sectors, and were neither prepared nor able to devote the resources to defend their U.S.-destined business at all costs. Thus FedEx and UPS quickly captured share, and DHL USA grabbed a smaller piece of a rapidly growing outbound market, faster than international DHL could respond inbound. The tensions between U.S. and rest of world management around this issue typically arose when dedicated air capacity was proposed to service U.S. outbound, only to be rebuffed by international DHL not willing to share or be exposed to the costs of such capacity on the return leg.

It remains an interesting if somewhat academic hypothesis to contemplate the outcome of a more aggressive approach to U.S. inbound business: after all, the entry of FedEx and UPS also grew the market faster than DHL could achieve without competition; and the reality was that DHL lacked the capital to engage in such aggressive loss leadership. If DHL had been an Uber-like unicorn...

Chapter 14
Business Context—Competition Explodes

Competition? (What, Really?)

It may seem strange that we do not focus on competitors until our fourteenth chapter. While there were early emulators to DHL in the 70s, with the exception of the near-fatal intervention in DHL's infancy by Loomis as it sought to collaborate with the rulemakers to snuff out an upstart, competitors did not threaten nor greatly influence DHL's position as a global pioneer. Nor did they help that much. In the postal battles of the 70s in the U.S., Purolator, operating in the U.S. and Canada, was cooperative at the outset. But when FedEx got involved, they, unencumbered by international distance and customs processes, offered delivery within twelve hours as the timeframe which defined where exemption to the postal monopoly could be granted. Which would have left DHL's more challenging international delivery performance (for the most part, longer than twelve hours) still in breach. There was no solidarity in the industry start-up phase, and DHL bore the brunt of the regulatory battle on its own slender shoulders.

Finally, Strength Through Numbers

But in 1983, the International Courier Conference was formed to challenge the, at the time, aggressive pursuit of monopoly enforcement in Europe, led by the French and German post offices. The ICC was comprised of DHL, Gelco Courier Services, IML Air Couriers, Purolator Courier Corporation, Securicor Air Couriers, TNT/Skypak, and World Courier. Gelco was an offshoot of the former Loomis and was acquired by FedEx later in the decade; IML (later to be acquired by UPS) was a UK-based firm with a niche into West Africa and specifically Nigeria; Purolator was ultimately acquired by Canada Post; Securicor, as has been mentioned, sold its express courier customer base to DHL; World Courier was a niche operator out of New York specializing in servicing the New York banks; and TNT Skypak was the newly-merged number two to DHL after TNT acquired IPEC. Not a very stable force, more of a motley crew, as subsequent events were to prove, but according to their deposition on European postal monopolies: "these seven couriers include

https://doi.org/10.1515/9781501507557-017

the major international couriers operating on an intercontinental scale" (Note the absence of the term "global.")[1]

Of all these operators, TNT and DHL alone had substance, with TNT being substantially larger overall because of its dominance of the Australian domestic market and its position in the overnight European trucking market. There were other niche players operating in different segments such as the Dutch XP, and the Japan based OCS (Overseas Courier Services) which specialized in servicing Japanese nationals working overseas with a steady supply of home newspapers. But the fact that we are already talking about segments indicates a certain adolescence, if not maturity, in the industry as various players tried their hand at getting things delivered faster than before.

But in Context

If you took the industry as a whole, and defined express to include domestic markets, then DHL was a small player at this stage, because the vast majority of express movements occurred within the United States, and there two players dominated, Federal Express and UPS. United Parcel Service has so far been below the radar, but that is because its origins and focus (dating back to 1927) were up until quite recently on intra-state deliveries by road. UPS had over the years overcome its own regulatory barriers which had been in place to protect inter-state freight movements as the exclusive domain of the railways. And then in the early 80s it started to respond to the FedEx threat by moving up market with an overnight service. The sole exception to this focus on intra and then interstate had been a 1976 entry into Germany, with the acquisition of a German domestic road freight business offering three–four day service within Germany. But in terms of number of shipments handled, UPS was the sleeping giant, with a much smaller FedEx still dwarfing all the other international players put together. A third player also emerged in the U.S., Airborne Express, which succeeded or succumbed to the inevitability of the number three position domestically and became known as the lowest-priced, no-frills option, thereby making DHL's effort to get to ten percent market share all that much tougher. Especially when TNT acquired an eighteen percent stake in Airborne. DHL's entry into the U.S. domestic market was, with hindsight, not the best of timing, but when else was it to be done? FedEx had

---

1 James I. Campbell, *The Rise of Global Delivery Firms: A Case Study in International Regulatory Reform*, Washington, D.C., JCampbell Press, 2001.

captured the overnight market with its "absolutely, positively, overnight" promise, had challenged the postal service directly with a 200-gram "letter" product, and thus the new entrants were left to compete on price. FedEx's reaction to the entry of UPS, Airborne, Purolator, Gelco and finally DHL, was to up the ante and offer guaranteed delivery before 10:30 a.m. the next day. The price collapse which followed was great for customers, but only UPS prospered, with its low-cost ground network able to absorb the downward price pressure.

Thus by the mid-80s DHL's late 1970s dominance had to be qualified by describing the niche which it occupied. An important niche, but a niche nonetheless, and while dominant in the international express sector, it had multiple concerns: technological substitution; the entry into the international market by one or both the U.S. giants, and the potential for the road integrators to move upstream.

And all of these threats were real, if not simultaneous. Hence the concurrent investments during this period which nearly sent DHL broke several times; U.S. domestic, Europe overnight, UK road haul, not to mention the foray into next generation fax and telecommunications.

Those Pesky Airlines Again

It wasn't just these competitors scrapping for the prize. The airlines, seeing that ultimately DHL would invest in its own air capacity, and frustrated by the operating methodology of onboard couriers, thought they ought to have a go as well. British Airways launched Speedbird, KLM joined forces with Jaap Mulder to form XP, Aer Lingus tried something with Securicor and many others tried. It was understandable from the airline perspective, that, as they controlled the belly space in their aircraft, they could provide the airport to airport part of the service at a lower cost than DHL, and therefore undercut on price. But what they underestimated was both the criticality and the complexity of being consistent on the ground. In this context, DHL and its focused competitors understood and owned the last mile, and the difference between DHL and those competitors was the culture, the culture, the culture.

DHL, in response, was busy building partnerships with each national carrier, to ensure capacity and schedules aligned with customer demand. Without a dominant nationality, DHL was able to position itself as local in every environment, and the default partner in each country was the national carrier. Not always reciprocated, of course, and often national carriers would both partner and compete (the beginnings of co-opetition).

The "Empires" Try to Strike Back

Those airfreight forwarders who tried to compete also had the formula wrong. Being experts at customs and dispatch was no substitute for daily door-to-door and total control. And the post offices also fancied themselves as players, with or without monopoly protection. The large European post offices, UK Post, and the U.S. Postal Service all entered the express market, but again, at this early stage lacked a coordinated approach for international traffic. Thus by 1986 the landscape was confused and confusing, but DHL's position as global leader of the international market segment was undisputed.

But FedEx Strikes First

And then FedEx flew into Paris in 1985, with its U.S. domestic model which added ownership of the aircraft to the definition of total control, as well as an ability and intent to capture more data through the barcode and put DHL to the technology, as well as the marketing, sword.

FedEx's approach to going international was to acquire local businesses and thereby shorten the race. So, they were able to avoid the comparatively arduous approach taken by DHL over fifteen years. Their move which made the most impact was the purchase of Flying Tigers, an all-freight airline which had emerged from the original Tigers' operations in Asia in World War II. Flying Tigers had one major asset, which surpassed the not-inconsiderable physical airplane assets, that being landing rights. The rights included fifth freedom rights (the right to carry passengers and freight from your home county to another, and also be able to add passengers and freight from that country to a third, and so on) which were in those days precious and closely regulated by each national agency. One of the prizes was access to Japan, which meant that Asia could be serviced with a stopover in Tokyo or Osaka. This was a deal which Larry and Pat Lupo had conceived and attempted, but FedEx pre-empted those efforts. Likewise, FedEx acquired Gelco, and, in another aggressive move, acquired the DHL agent in the Caribbean, threatening service to the twenty-four countries added to DHL's network earlier in the decade.

This was a serious threat to DHL. In the domestic market, FedEx was cleaning up, and also had launched its own version of electronic substitution, called Zap-Mail. Now the battle became global. Po Chung recalls that Fred Smith, the FedEx CEO, had asked how long DHL people could continue to fire in the marketplace. Clearly, he felt that DHL's soft asset base, meaning its people and its culture, would be no substitute for the power of FedEx's hard asset, engineered approach, and would sooner or later burn out. Po's response was to the effect that DHL people could continue to fire for a long long time.

And Starts to Force the Pace

One aspect of the FedEx business model which did cause immediate problems to DHL was FedEx's approach to data capture and positive tracking. The FedEx model of hub-and-spoke, within a single customs domain, meant that packages could be scanned in and out of the hub, as well as at pick-up and delivery. They had invested heavily in barcode technology and scanners to support their overnight-before-10:30 a.m. service guarantee, and create a powerful customer expectation that packages could be tracked as well as traced. They took that expectation and perception with them internationally, and used it to contrast with DHL's comparatively loose system of control, with, in reality, just a tracing, or reactive, approach to backing up the service promise. This ignored the more complex data gathering requirements of moving packages through diverse customs channels. FedEx did not have to capture content and value within the US.

It didn't matter that in reality FedEx had a big task converting its acquisitions to its technology and business model. U.S. customers were told that the FedEx service would be the same everywhere, so pressure was on DHL to provide the same level of perceived control internationally. Many of DHL's international customers also used FedEx within the U.S., and most likely to a greater extent. Hence DHL was on the back foot. Debate raged within the operational teams across the DHL world as to the real benefits of "positive tracking" versus the more economical "exception tracking," i.e. only capturing data on shipments which were late, or about to be late, because of a missed connection. After all, DHL's service performed to expectation ninety-five percent of the time.

This argument was to be resolved first by the power of customer expectation and an increasing requirement by customs services for more information sooner, to respond to the courier industry's pressure for faster clearance times. A perfect storm, and DHL was obliged to step up to a higher level of data capture, which both improved the perception of control expected by customers, as well as supported the growth of the parcel business. Thank you FedEx!

The Enemy of My Enemy Can be My Friend

With the arrival of both FedEx and UPS into the international arena, the hard work DHL had done in building relationships and partnerships with the commercial carriers began to pay off. FedEx now became a bigger threat and the way to counter FedEx and UPS was to partner with DHL. Thus Cathay Pacific in Hong Kong became the airline partner for much of Asia. Sabena in Belgium became the partner for the first transatlantic cargo flight. There were many other examples, such as the airline operating within Saudi Arabia (SNAS), Russow Air, an early partner during the Frankfurt hub era, and EAT, a Belgian airline which DHL subsequently acquired.

While DHL could afford to be just a little complacent about competition in 1979, the environment had clearly and rapidly changed by the middle of the 80s.

Chapter 15
Regulatory Battles

Postal Battles Heat Up

By 1980, DHL was operating in almost every continent, and had encountered regulatory barriers all along the way. The most threatening of these battles came from the post offices, belligerent and indignant in the belief that DHL was illegal because it contravened their legal monopoly to carry letters. Although the problems encountered in the U.S., Hong Kong and Europe were serious, the early skirmishes were typically ignored until they had to be addressed, due to seizures by customs authorities, harassment of customers or outright legal action. DHL weathered the early storms, and in doing so built up a caseload of precedent and argument, both legal (the law is an ass!), economic (DHL as an integral part of the new global business framework), as well as political. DHL customers supported the fight, and in most cases the authorities backed down, if only to fight again another day. In Hong Kong, a change in the law was defeated, but this was the only clear-cut victory. The U.S. battle was ongoing, but important points of principle were established in terms of defining the core differences between an express courier service and a postal service, in organizational as well as service respects. In Europe, the Swiss and Italian authorities relied on sixty-year-old statutes authorizing "breaches" as long as domestic postage rates were also applied. In Italy, this was administered loosely.

But any notion that the issues were being overcome by 1979 was quickly negated by aggressive action on the parts of the French and German post offices in the early 80s, with other aggressive activity in Singapore, Korea, Africa, Argentina to name but a few examples. DHL managers came to expect that at some point in time the postal issue would rear its ugly head, and it wasn't until the end of the decade that the emphasis shifted from regulatory pressure to competitive pressure with the emergence of express postal offerings. In the meantime, the industry grew up to an extent, with the formation of the International Courier Conference in Geneva in 1983, and combined resources to support what had been up until then a practically solo effort by DHL and its various counsels to fight for the industry. This organization and its initiatives arrived also at a time when the European authorities began to take a look at postal laws in the context of the Treaty of Rome, signed some twenty-five years before, in an effort to promote competition across the European Economic Union. The singular victory of the 80s, however, was the suspension of the British postal monopoly in late 1981, a move

https://doi.org/10.1515/9781501507557-018

which typified the independent nature of the British as well as the reformist zeal of Prime Minister Thatcher.

The postal monopoly in the UK was under pressure toward the end of the 70s because of poor service, and interestingly the focus was domestic not international services per se. When the Conservatives under Margaret Thatcher swept to power in 1980 on a platform of deregulation, smaller government and more competition in public services, one of the earliest targets was the Post and Telecommunications Act, which separated the postal and telecommunications agencies. New regulations signaled the right of the minister to suspend the monopoly for carriage of urgent letters. This he duly did in late 1981, and the mechanism he used was price, an expedient method of overcoming resistance from the incumbent and its employee unions. The monopoly was suspended for carriage of any letter for which the charge exceeded £1 (One British Pound), until 2006. By this time, it was assumed that much more of the Post Office's activities would have been priced at or over that limit by virtue of inflation (the £1 threshold not being subject to inflationary adjustment). This move immediately legalized all of DHL's activities overnight, and of course DHL was prepared, immediately launching its first-ever television campaign which coincided with the global efforts to build brand and awareness begun at the DHL conference that year in Athens.

The Europeans, however, were not at all interested in deregulation in spite of the Treaty of Rome, designed to progressively promote the removal of customs and other trade barriers, including competitive barriers, signed way back in 1957. In 1980, the French Post Office forced a licensing of international couriers by way of a tax based on fifteen percent of the fees charged by their own fledgling domestic express mail service Postadex. And two years later, it further tightened the noose by insisting that couriers only operate from Paris, the presumed international gateway, and that forwarding beyond Paris be conducted through the postal services. Presumably the express service was assumed to be making a fifteen percent profit! Concurrently, Germany attempted to control the industry by way of requiring the couriers to advertise the fact that they would not carry letters and would in fact decline to carry any items in contravention. This unworkable solution was also offered in the light of a declaration that Deutsche Post's own international express offering would soon be sufficiently fast that it would obviate the need for private couriers.

What was significant here was that these two major postal authorities, in Europe's largest economies, were no longer brandishing the postal monopoly as an existential threat to DHL. Instead, at least in their eyes, they were attempting to offer imaginative ways to allow the industry to operate and respect the spirit if not the intent of the law. There was an unexplained hesitancy to test the monopoly provisions in a court of law. Conversely, DHL prepared for a legal challenge with some anxiety and equal hesitancy not to provoke what might be an unacceptably negative ruling and therefore precedent. It was a game of shadow boxing around the issues, with, on the one hand, DHL putting forward economic arguments, such as the unprecedented study commissioned by the Bureau d'Informations et Previsions Economique (BIPE). BIPE is a semi-official research organization in France, which argued that several of France's export-oriented industrial sectors were using such services for transporting paper-based materials such as technical drawings, in ways and for purposes which the postal law never envisaged. On the other hand, the post offices were protecting their rights to regulate and price as opposed to replace courier activities. But, of course, it was an expensive, one-sided boxing match in that DHL's meagre resources were up against the might of two incumbent national institutions. Worse, DHL was neither French nor German, and their managers were foreigners who spoke only English!

Two things happened concurrently to turn the tide. First, the European Commission decided to take an active interest in national postal monopolies in the context of the Treaty. While the French initially dismissed their intervention, the Germans were much more sensitive to the spirit of the European Union, and much more economically interested as well. Second, DHL was finally able to create an industry body to present a collective voice in support of the efforts to win a legitimate place in the world of international commerce. As mentioned earlier, in 1983, the International Courier Conference was formed, convening for the first time in Geneva. Later the name was changed to International Express Carriers Conference (IECC) in deference to what was already an expanding industry which also included parcels and was showing signs of multi-modal integration. For the next several years the industry had a common voice and a common purpose, picking up on DHL's lead of avoiding direct confrontation and concentrating on economic studies and arguments, as well as opportunistically picking up on peripheral political issues such as the French Post Office's—no doubt unintended— discrimination against the economic prospects of the provinces by trying to limit the geographical reach of the international couriers to Paris.

In Asia, the Singapore Post Office intervened via customs with seizures of DHL material in 1980. In this case the authorities backed down after pressure from customers, including the local U.S. Chamber of Commerce. In South Africa, an early battle was won on the basis of the price differential which clearly existed between postal charges and DHL fees, and in Nigeria, the Federation of Chambers of Commerce congratulated the courier industry for their courage and resilience in operating in such a chaotic environment while excoriating the local Postal Service for their ineptitude. But it was in Tunisia that DHL met its match. During the late 70s and early 80s the UPU had been urging its constituent members to excise the cancer that was DHL before it was too late. Those entreaties were echoed in the regional meetings such as the Arab Postal Union and the Pan African Postal Union (which prompted the Nigerian outburst). By 1980, in most of the Middle East, the strength of DHL's local partners was sufficient to foreclose any pre-emptive strike by local postal authorities, but in Tunisia, with its French-based law, the situation was different. The head of the Tunisian Post Office, attending an Arab Postal Union meeting, boasted to his colleagues that DHL did not exist nor ever would exist in his country. As it turned out, DHL had been operating in Tunis for over a year by this time, under a license granted by the Ministry of Transport. The Tunisian Post Master General was therefore aghast when he saw the DHL sign on a suburban villa which served as office and residence for the expat DHL manager. Approximately a year later, having done his homework and prepared his ground, the official acted and closed down DHL's operation in a flurry of red tape which took years and years to undo. A similar story unfolded in Morocco, no doubt inspired by the belligerence of the French Post office. For the time being, DHL considered these markets too small to warrant a head on battle, and patience proved the ultimate virtue in due course.

By the mid-80s, two significant developments emerged from the typically chaotic (or opportunistic) as well as pejorative nature of the relationship and interaction between postal authorities and courier services. First, the principles which focused the debate in the U.S. in the late 70s took hold elsewhere, namely that the nature of the service offered as opposed to the content of what was carried became the issue. Arguing about what constituted a letter became a circular, almost unwinnable argument without the test of a summary court ruling, and both sides were reluctant to put their positions to such a test. So, the focus of the debate and the language used shifted significantly to begin to define the preconditions for a relaxation of monopoly conditions, or a means of maintaining control in a fast changing commercial environment. Typically, the French opted for the maintenance of control position, but found a way through by introducing a definition of urgency which included, naturally enough, speed, but also the notion of guarantee and administrative control. In other words, courier services were different in that they were prepared to guarantee their service and at all times knew where the consignment was through detailed management and administrative control. This was the gist of the ruling by the French authorities in 1985 which rescued them from the political consequences of trying to limit service to Paris as a point of entry and export. It also signaled the second development, which was that post offices were beginning to organize competitive offerings of their own; hence the initial German approach to slowing down the development of the private sector services while their own service had a chance to catch up.

The next phase in the regulatory battle over postal laws occurred as the battle moved from express to bulk remail. This was another form of arbitrage whereby bulk mail was consolidated and moved by express companies from one postal jurisdiction to another, and entered into destination countries' postal services for final delivery, or in some cases further international fulfilment through the postal network. This hybrid service took advantage of different countries' domestic postal rates, especially in cases where exchange rate differences translated into savings. For example, for companies sending out notices to foreign shareholders it was, in some cases, cheaper to bulk the letters into single consignments, have a courier company ship as one consignment, and pay domestic postal rates at destination. This worked just like the telex store and forward service described earlier but was even more threatening to the UPU because the terminal dues system used for calculating compensation between post offices was being ignored and undermined. Bulk remail traffic was not captured by the system, so origin post offices would not receive income for mail originating in their jurisdictions. Destination post offices enjoyed the full benefit of domestic revenue from this "imported" mail which was often higher than they would have received as terminal dues. These post offices were tacit if not active collaborators with the courier firms in attracting such new sources of revenue. In short, the remail business caused as much confusion and dissension among members of the UPU as it had fostered unity in the previous discussions against couriers. Over the next few years the IECC fought an exhausting fight against the UPU and its sub-committees over this issue, to the extent that DHL took a back-row seat, as remail wasn't the highest of its priorities and the other members of the IECC had a much larger commercial stake in the product. Besides, remail wasn't going to change the world.

However, this protracted battle was often fought by member postal regimes with fundamental conflicts in that many of them were active participants in the activity. Solidarity around core UPU principles were increasingly being observed in the breach. At the same time, post offices explicitly and globally embarked on a "can't beat 'em, let's join 'em" strategy and began to launch their own coordinated international express services, as well as participating in the remail game of arbitrage. They were effectively using their statutory position in defense of their monopoly as an exercise in buying time to gain competitive advantage. In 1989 a group of twenty post offices formed the International Postal Corporation with the objective of providing a coordinated express service to compete directly with the private express companies. They chose Brussels as their coordinating center. This effort proved to be short-lived and the early 90s saw direct investment into the express industry with five European Post Offices taking a direct stake in TNT. Subsequently the Dutch Post Office, newly privatized, took control. The express industry had truly arrived.

It is important to note at this point the clear differences in the various responses from individual countries in those early years and how they split between a liberal and an authoritarian view based on their legal code. The maritime/continental argument about cultural predisposition to the global service industry clearly wins points on the issue of postal deregulation, as the most permissive environments in the mid-80s were clearly to be found in the British Commonwealth countries. Conversely the most aggressive defenders of monopoly power had a legal structure based on the Napoleonic Code (see Chapter 9). The Dutch, as we also see in our discussions about taxation, proved again a notable exception to the maritime/continental rule, being a colonizing, sea-faring nation with a distinctly continental regulatory framework.

Progress with Customs

The use of onboard couriers had enabled DHL and competitors to get around the complex processes and entrenched interests which characterized the clearance of airfreight or indeed any cargo shipment whether by air, land or sea. It also gave customs authorities a rationale for tolerating the differences in treatment of a package of documents whether the package was tendered for clearance in the passenger hall or in the airfreight terminal. But, as we have seen, the astonishing growth of DHL and its rivals was causing problems of congestion in the baggage halls as well as complaints from the traditional forwarding industry about the upstarts getting more favorable treatment. It was especially clear in the latter case when DHL and the courier industry had their sights set on taking a slice out of the freight market through their small parcel offerings.

In 1986, the Customs Cooperation Council (CCC), an international body of national customs services, was specifically asked by its members to examine the phenomena of urgent or express consignments. The IECC eagerly grasped this opportunity to argue that there was a need to completely shift the paradigm for clearances of urgent consignments, and provided evidence that these consignments were different in a number of significant ways. First, they were typically small and of low commercial value. Second, they were different from traditional cargo in that for the most part they were shipper-initiated. The current customs clearance processes and protocols were driven by the fact that most of the goods being imported were at the request of the consignee or receiver, and therefore the knowledge base of what was coming and how it should be classified for customs duties resided with the receiver, i.e. within the country of import. In the case of urgent consignments, however, knowledge of content and value was typically held by the shipper. Finally, therefore, it was more about the nature of the service being provided, which was a different service from that provided by traditional airfreight forwarders, than it was about the mode of transport used, e.g. on-board couriers and passenger baggage. Besides, most courier firms used airfreight as well as on-board couriers.

The work which started in 1986 was painstakingly slow in terms of gaining consensus among the members of the CCC, many of whom were under pressure from the airfreight forwarder community not to give special status to the express companies. But while dramatic reform was not possible, the arguments for and against were now in the public domain, thereby assuring a certain legitimacy to the case for change. And the insignificant consensus which emerged around building Memorandums of Understanding (MOU) at the country level between customs and couriers actually bore the most fruit. The express companies argued that the cost of processing clearance formalities and collecting duties below a certain value was higher than the revenue actually collected. On the other hand, customs authorities were most concerned about contraband and drugs. Constructive discussions around these issues under an MOU framework enabled relationships to grow and the more contentious aspects of the reform program to be put to one side in favor of pragmatic win-win solutions. Recognizing the logic of not collecting duties on low value items was matched by an equal concern by the carriers to reduce the risk that their services were being targeted for use by drug traffickers. The request by customs for more information, sooner, was also accepted by the industry as a necessary evil, because it also supported the growing demand from customers for more proactive tracking.

So, conflict turned to cooperation. The progressive acceptance by customs across the world of the principle of de-minimus values, i.e. a value threshold below which it was uneconomic to process and collect duties, did more than anything to stimulate the express parcel business and enable DHL to escape the limitations of being a single-product business. Recognition of the special status of goods which were typically small in volume and low in extrinsic value, but high in intrinsic value, i.e. time-sensitive, also brought customs around to supporting the special facilities which were now popping up at the bigger airports. And the extra data captured which supported the dual requirements of customs and customers, also drove information systems development which in turn supported the growing discipline of logistics. Greater, real-time visibility into where goods were located in increasingly complex supply chains meant greater efficiencies in coordinating sourcing, manufacturing and distribution. It also meant that surges in demand, or unforeseen pressure on supply, were captured sooner as information and intelligence were communicated throughout the chain using the newly unleashed power of the internet.

What we are seeing here is the maturing of a new worldwide industry, led by DHL, with a common sense of purpose and a common set of arguments which pointed to the fact that existing postal and customs laws were anachronistic. These aging regulations no longer served their purpose in the face of a rapid rise of international trade and the accompanying recognition that speed-to-market was a key competitive advantage. While regulatory reform was far from over, DHL was no longer under existential threat. On the contrary it was now an accepted fact of global life that DHL and its industry colleagues were now a necessity for businesses doing business on a global or international scale.

Tax, Cashflows and Blocked Funds

As indicated in the previous chapter on the regulatory environment, DHL in the 70s had no formal means of moving cash from one jurisdiction to another. DHL's simple proposition was for the shipper, or sender, to pay one price for the entire transaction, door-to-door. This contrasted with alternative means, other than by conventional post, where the freight forwarder process was fragmented with lots of small invoices being generated along the way, some paid by the sender, some paid by the receiver. True, if a customer used the post office, they paid everything at origin. But post offices had the cumbersome terminal dues systems to sort out compensation for costs incurred when there was no direct revenue. DHL, at the beginning, had no such system. DHL countries who had little direct responsibility to pay for airline costs, perhaps only for the first, short, outbound sector to the transfer hub, quickly built up big cash balances from collecting the full price of the service from their customers. France was a typical example of a country actually paying just a fraction of its total costs of final delivery, whereas the countries or cities where the transfer hubs were located paid for more airline costs than were reflected by their own outbound traffic. London was a case in point here. Similarly, countries with imbalances between pickups and deliveries had contrasting cash flows. Those countries with more outbound than inbound also generated cash, as there were less resources required for delivery; for those countries with more inbound than outbound, there was often a cash drain, in that local receipts might not be sufficient to cover all costs, particularly in the start-up phase. Furthermore, in some countries where cash balances were high, there were exchange controls. It was not just a simple process transferring funds, with or without an invoice describing what was owed and why. Many developing countries put huge controls over the processes of paying for services incurred outside of the country in foreign currency. Their priorities were typically to conserve their foreign exchange to acquire capital goods, not services. And so the prospect of excess cash being "blocked" and unavailable for use became a real issue.

The Dutch Sandwich

Now the tax lawyers got busy, trying to devise a mechanism for a business model and a modus operandi which defied conventional views of how business was done across borders, how revenue was recognized, and under whose jurisdiction sat any tax liability.

Once again, the solution, known as the Dutch Sandwich, was elegant in its simplicity. In the early days of fighting the US CAB, one consequence was the separation of DHL Corporation (USA) from international (DHL International Hong Kong). After looking at taxation and foreign exchange regulations worldwide, a further split then occurred, between DHL International (DHLI), which owned and operated the DHL international network outside of the USA, and the entities which owned and operated the local company in each country. DHLI became responsible for all costs incurred in an international environment. i.e. all costs associated with air transport and intermediate airport hub and transfer operations, while the local DHL company, owned by different shareholders, was responsible for ground operations, i.e. pick-up and delivery. These companies earned the right to the use of the DHL name by performing consistently regardless of whether the package was inbound or outbound. The simplicity in this arrangement translated into an equally simple contract between the local and the international entity. The local company would be guaranteed a profit of 10 percent of its costs, and the difference between that figure (costs for outbound and inbound, plus ten percent) and receipts from sending customers, was paid to the international network for fulfilment. This arrangement avoided the costly process of cost accounting for each individual shipment, the process generally used by freight forwarders, albeit for larger shipping units, and made necessary also by the fact that the supply chain was full of disparate players, each wanting their piece of the action. It also avoided the issue of imbalance (a country delivering more pieces than it was picking up) as well as ownership of the customer, most of whom were multinational anyway. It is important here to distinguish between ownership of the customer from an accounting perspective, and responsibility for servicing the customer, which became a separate issue later on when multinationals started to insist on global contracts.

The Dutch Sandwich appellation arose from the fact that the Netherlands provided a tax jurisdiction most accommodating for novel approaches to global business such as DHL was proposing. Hence DHL I (Hong Kong) set up its network operating subsidiary as an offshore Dutch company, and the local entities were also predominantly owned by a Dutch holding company (unless local laws made it obligatory for one hundred percent local ownership). This turned out to be an elegantly simple solution, and one which most developed countries found both generous (to the local company) and pragmatic, given the complexity of the network and each package's individual journey (which could be different on different days of the week). Essentially the risk of the business was borne by the international network, and all the local company needed to do to maintain its contract and ensure a profit, was to perform efficiently. Incentives elegantly aligned!

But not all countries saw simple as good, and the plus-ten percent operating agreement was viewed with suspicion in many environments whose culture, legal and tax codes were not predisposed to global commerce. In short, this was another challenge for the lawyers and tax advisors. For example, in French-speaking Africa, whose currencies were tied to the French franc, there were no foreign exchange controls per se, but neither the tax advisors nor the authorities (whose views the advisors interpreted) could or would trust the costs-plus formula. So the solution to this problem was to treat the handling fee as the local company income, and the weight rates as the fee representing the international costs which would then be transferred to the network, less airline costs incurred locally. Dalsey's elegantly simple pricing structure became enshrined for tax purposes. Such a causal link could not last, of course, as competition forced discounting of the handling fee, and the bespoke operating agreement did not compensate for imbalances between inbound and outbound. So it was not sustainable, but pragmatic in the short term.

Value-added tax also presented a challenge. In the French legal and tax environment, value-added tax was focused on service, and in fact the tax was specifically named as such (Taxe sur les prestations de services, or TPS). In most environments, an exemption was easily obtained based on the argument that the entire DHL offering was one integrated international service which didn't distinguish between the local pick-up or delivery components as distinct services. But in the French environments the handling fee stood out, and the operating agreement reinforced the notion that this pricing component was for local services.

Hence in some cases VAT, or TPS, or GST ended up being levied on the monthly handling fee, in order to be pragmatic.

But at least in these environments, money could move (the former French colonies all had a currency freely convertible to the French franc). In others, where strict exchange controls existed, because the country was short of foreign exchange, cash just built up, effectively blocked. Hence the choice of Athens (this is before the euro) for the first global meeting was specifically made in order to use up blocked funds. Other countries with similarly blocked funds were used for conferences (but only the African region would go to Nigeria), and efforts were also made to pay airline costs from those countries, or to manufacture supplies. But the airlines themselves might have the same issues with getting local receipts for long-distance travel appropriately repatriated, and therefore limit the extent to which DHL could use its local currency for flights beyond the first destination. Also, the fact that exchange controls were in place in the first place meant that the economy of the blocked-fund country was not structured to effectively compete internationally, hence stuff made in those countries wasn't necessarily of a sufficiently high standard for global use. This issue was not going to be solved overnight. In many of the blocked-fund countries, it wasn't just the DHL business model creating confusion or mistrust, it might also be because the country just didn't have foreign exchange. Certainly, the notion of spending precious foreign exchange on a service agreement as opposed to the purchase of tangible goods was also a barrier; as was the prevalence of corruption where local middlemen might take a very substantial clip in getting an application for foreign exchange through the bureaucracy. DHL's perspective was that the network was the key: if customers wanted DHL to do business in a particular country, then DHL would persevere. Having funds blocked, or experiencing long delays in getting paid, was one of the costs of doing business globally.

Chapter 16
Cultural Dynamics

Heroism

What drives people to risk their lives to keep a business going during war, civil unrest or natural disaster? Ask the two courier/managers in Tehran, who maintained a DHL service during the Iranian Revolution which deposed the Shah in 1979. Or the team in Beirut, who drove the "Green Line" between East and West Beirut, a road notorious for its snipers, throughout the Lebanese Civil War in the late 70s and early 80s. Or the folk in DHL Mexico, who kept their service going during the catastrophic earthquake of 1985, and offered free telex services so people could send messages to loved ones abroad. Fast forward into the 90s, and similar stories abound, in Yemen, Saudi Arabia, Kuwait during the Gulf War, Africa, the Balkans (some deliveries mind you, took four years, kept safe by a courier during the long years of the Sarajevo siege). These extreme examples are typical of an esprit de corps which existed all around the DHL world and which resurrected the old Pony Express maxim, "the mail must go through!" with its incumbent values of fearlessness and dedication. This was a common set of values and commitment, and it didn't matter where you were in the world, what language you spoke, and what your role was, fulfilling the promise made somewhere else in the world, in another language, by someone you might never meet was something that you just did, because the service was so important and so valued by customers. Especially in the most chaotic of situations. How does such a culture emerge?

It Wasn't Just the Cowboys

We have seen how this powerful culture and commitment to service was born through the examples of the founders and early managers, and instilled and nurtured into every new DHL employee, not unlike a master/apprentice model. It was more than just a job, it was something akin to a movement, a belief, a crusade against the forces of resistance protecting the status quo. And it was personal, not just in the context of life stage, excitement and experience that came from dealing with the world on a daily basis, but in meeting like-minded people from different cultures and backgrounds. It was also personal in that a service failure, a shipment delayed, temporarily lost, a pick-up missed, a deadline missed—all of

https://doi.org/10.1515/9781501507557-019

these slip-ups which inevitably occurred in the maelstrom of daily activity were taken personally by those involved. It was an emotional issue dealing with failure, and letting the customer and the network down.

But it was, of course, also fun; and it was gratifying to be trusted, with the minimum of guidance from above, to do the right thing, even if that sometimes meant not doing it right. Being trusted meant that it was natural to delegate the trust in turn, and hence the early hectic expansion of DHL was underpinned by this adhesive of trust. Mobility, youthful exuberance and intelligence were also the ingredients by which DHL got lucky with its early workforce of itinerant colonials, many of whom had university degrees in all disciplines, *excluding* business. In fact, the predominant academic background was the liberal arts.

Dave's cowboys also enjoyed a common cultural heritage which could be defined as maritime, but also exemplified the more permissive, bottom-up approach to organizing society and its constituent parts as embedded in the English code of law and legal practice. But, as the examples above attest, there was no natural monopoly accorded to the Anglo-Saxon way of life and thinking when it came to performing the service with such passion and dedication. Surely, then, the maritime culture was simply the channel via which this viral phenomenon was disseminated globally, to affect and infect all cultures. Dave's cowboys were the disciples for this global creed. The expatriate leader inspired the local recruits, and was also prepared to take risks, in a business context, and stand up to authority, in a regulatory context, in a way that the locals might be more reticent to do.

Growing Up

Tension in the relationship between expatriate and local played out as DHL matured. It became necessary to codify the genetic traits of what had worked so far in "seat of the pants" fashion, into a culture and set of values which applies universally and sustainably. When Bill Walden set up the regions and also brought in older, reputedly wiser heads to fill skills gaps, he was careful to nurture the strengths of the independent nature of local participation in the global DHL crusade, and not dumb it down through layers of bureaucracy. Hence the philosophical statements in the International Herald Tribune, paying tribute to the advantages of decentralization, sentiments which became clarion calls as each region freely began to establish its own identity within a network family. This transition from (relative) chaos to (relative) order was not without consequence. There was understandable resistance from some at this sudden arrival of a layer of management which represented just as much a generational gap as it did a welcome injection of wisdom and experience. Some good people had their wings clipped, and some good people moved on, but in retrospect the overall transition, the introduction of discipline, structure and focus, was achieved not just through trust, but more importantly, respect. Bill and his band of older cohorts for the most part treated the young leaders with respect, and often considerable patience. The respect issue was critical, as the inevitable tension occurred between a "just do it" mentality, which the young operational group implicitly if not explicitly espoused as a virtue, and the more thoughtful, risk-aware approach of seasoned professionals, raising awareness of the law of unintended consequence. It was a more rational and considered approach to what hitherto might have been credited to "Murphy's law," or, as was seen later in the vernacular, "shit happens." It was, after all, a precarious moment in DHL's short history, and the outcome of ill-conceived actions might be fatal.

Bill's approach was also respectful, and sometimes fatherly, especially when young managers left themselves wide open to huge gaps in logic, or were seduced by the hyperbole of a grand assumption. Such as the assertion by one manager that TNT Skypak's forty percent market share was of no import, and an indication of them being in disarray. At that point, often in the formality of a conference, Bill would adjust his glasses and beg a young man to explain to an old man just how that could possibly be! "Could you give an old man a little comfort and explain how that works?" was an oft-used expression. The respectful nature of the leadership quickly turned to intolerance, however, if incompetence or poor grasp of the numbers were exposed. And the all-consuming quest for knowledge about what was going on, and who was doing what to whom, was frequently curtailed by an explanation of the difference between what people wanted to know, and what they needed to know. DHL's successful internal jungle drums, resonating through the grapevine, had to adjust their beat to that which was needed to be known.

This transition from wanting to know, to needing to know, also took place in a broader context of externalizing DHL's focus to better understand the broader market. What drove customers in terms of a comprehensive set of requirements as opposed to simply wanting service to this or that place? It was not only the pick-up and delivery which mattered, it was the entire experience, including the image projected visually and verbally, and especially over the phone. Structured customer service was a new discipline; call centers could make calls as well as answer them. Sales could be effectively made using the telephone, to complement the sales call as a lower-cost option and broader geographical reach.

In short, it was time to move DHL from an operational focus to an explicit market driven focus, which of course required a more detailed understanding of and respect for competitor dynamics, hitherto dismissed as insignificant and unworthy. All this, within the relatively new context of what gets measured, gets managed. An emphasis on key performance indicators and management reporting constrained the hitherto uncontrolled operational leadership style to create a hybrid of "ready, fire, aim" and "ready, aim, fire." One didn't want to extinguish the unbridled enthusiasm which kept the wheels of expansion rolling, but harnessing it was essential to survival. Bill used Drucker a lot, and urged his young charges to continue to innovate and treat risk as an obstacle, not a barrier. "It is far more important to know the right thing to do, than to know what to avoid doing" was a Drucker quote Bill used at the Athens meeting.[1] Putting a philosophical as well as a structural context over the young business was a revelation to many young managers who might once have frowned at the prospect of a business career.

In the early 80s, the function of Human Resources (HR) made its entry into the DHL lexicon as a consequence of this focus on more structure and discipline. However, the notion of people as assets was still very new, and the practitioners of the new human resource discipline were also new, and all too often people ended up in HR after less than distinguished efforts in other disciplines. These were the least impressive of the new organizational changes, in the views of the operational leaders, who were accustomed to moving people around like pawns on a chessboard, and reluctant to be diverted from that view. Besides, there was enough new stuff to absorb like marketing and budgets and cash flows without the further complication of people management.

It was also a challenge to young and relatively immature leaders to step up to a more formal approach to managing employees when the whole fabric of DHL was built around camaraderie and informality. It was a refreshingly egalitarian environment; everyone, including Bill, Dave and Po, was on a first-name basis; there might have been a leadership hierarchy, but it was not a social one. Even Larry was Larry, although he typically would respond by using just the surname, but that was accepted as idiosyncrasy which proved the rule that DHL was indeed like a family, and Larry was the brilliant black sheep. So, in this area of management skill, trust and respect still worked instead of structure and process. If an employee fit in, worked hard, and did the job, then any issues of an employment nature could be taken care of with an undocumented fireside or bar-side chat, and the next day everyone could be good mates again. But of course, it couldn't stay as simple and as one-sided as that forever.

---

1 Peter F. Drucker, *People and Performance*, Routledge, 2011, p. 109.

DHL Global Conference, Palm Springs, 1987

First DHL Global Conference, Athens, 1981

Some Contextual Frameworks

Po Chung, in his recent work on Service Leadership[2] has retrospectively identified what was going on here, in terms of an implicit and intuitive view of people management. From recruitment to development and the emergence of a leadership style and cadre, what differentiated DHL from others and underpinned the emergence of DHL as a global phenomenon? What was it that enabled a great idea to turn into a great and innovative service which resonated across national, language and cultural, as opposed to regulatory, barriers?

In Po's work, as he examines the characteristic leadership of a service business, he boils it down to a set of three principles: *competence, character and care.* Competence is a combination of at least functional and preferably also leadership competence. Character embodies the principles of business and personal integrity as well as trustworthiness. Care is predominantly about caring for others, empathy rather than sympathy, in the context of the people an employee works with. But it is also about caring about the service, and the passion which drives an emotional response to and personal responsibility for service failure.

While this was far from an explicit framework for how DHL functioned in the 80s, it does resonate. This was a new business and a new idea; competence grew with experience, and competence, as identified earlier, was shared on the job by people in a hurry with no thought let alone time for job protection. So, leadership competence in this context was also evident from an early stage. Later on, it might argue that one of the key competencies of a leader, that of hiring up, rather than down, was seeded by Bill bringing in the new skill sets and having these newcomers report to their young, operationally oriented new bosses. The successful young leaders who survived and thrived, learned to back themselves, to hire people with competencies which they themselves did not possess.

Character was definitely a factor, in that enormous responsibility for decisions was delegated, often out of practical necessity, but clearly that delegation engendered trust, and DHL in turn had good fortune to hire trustworthy, incorruptible people.

Care existed both in terms of the family nature of the global team, caring and looking out for each other, as well as the passion for service fulfilment, and the personal disappointment which came with service failure.

Another C could be added: collaboration was embedded as an integral part of the service, a promise made, a pick-up made in one country to be fulfilled in another. And it was reciprocated: "you deliver mine on time, and I'll deliver

---

2 Po Chung, *Service Reborn*, Lexingford Publishers, 2012

yours." The voluntary nature of collaboration arises from this core principle, in that by extension, DHL people looked after each other; they watched each other's back, and jumped in to help when problems arose.

The three or four "Cs" certainly captures much of what made DHL exceptional, and, with the "we never close" phenomena described at the beginning of this chapter, three more might be added: courage, conviction, and a just a smidgeon of craziness!

To use another, more contemporary framework, consider the release in 1982 of what has been to date the biggest-selling business book of all time. In the late 70s and early 80s, Peters and Waterman traveled the world interviewing major corporations about teams and organization in business. The resultant book, *In Search of Excellence*[3] turned management theory on its head by concentrating on the "soft," or less tangible attributes of success as opposed to the "hard" or numbers-driven view which prevailed at the time. DHL was not on their radar, but it would be fascinating to know what their view might have been had they attended the Athens conference or spent any time with DHL leaders. Essentially, they broke down their findings into eight themes or attributes which they found, if not consistently, at least concurrently across the forty-two successful multi-nationals which they identified:

- *A bias for action*: the "just do it," just get it done attitude. Getting on with the job in hand and not being distracted
- *Close to the customer*: learning from the people served by the business
- *Autonomy and entrepreneurship*: fostering innovation and nurturing "champions"
- *Productivity through people*: treating rank and file employees as a source of quality
- *Hands-on, values driven*: management philosophy that is visible through leaders walking around, being visible, walking the talk
- *Stick to the knitting*: staying focused on the business you know
- *Simple-form, lean staff*: adopting a minimalist approach to head office in terms of size and function
- *Simultaneous loose-tight properties*: being clear on what matters as standards, what needs to be standardized, and what freedoms to act exist and are encouraged.

---

3 Peterman, Thomas J. and Waterman, Robert H. *In Search of Excellence: Lessons from America's Best-Run Companies*. New York: Harper and Row, 1982.

This might have been the DHL bible had it been written at the time and one can easily cross reference each of the attributes as fundamental to DHL's culture and style. But at the time it would have been improbable if not impossible to articulate, such was the nature of the emergence which we identified at the close of the 70s, and which the Walden years served to nurture. Suffice it to say that the book became a management bible among the young DHL leaders, and many chose it as a platform from which to educate their growing workforce. At the same time, they were all a bit miffed that DHL hadn't been a case study for the book, such did the eight attributes resonate as a reflection of the way things were already being done.

And Perhaps a Modern Example of Another, More Natural Law, is in Play Here

In Chapter 9, we discussed DHL's emergence in biological terms. Adrian Bejan has recently proposed a new principle he calls the Constructal Law. It is a variation of a law of physics. It claims to unify the hitherto juxtaposed laws of "living" biology (Darwinian) with the laws of physics and thermodynamics and their "dead state" presumptions. It espouses design through natural processes as opposed to a creationist view of why nature is as it is. It takes river flows, trees, the human lung and blood system as examples of a natural tendency to optimize flow over time, following thermodynamic principles that currents tend to flow from high (pressure, altitude) to low. We propose, as one of our twelve powers, which summarize the key attributes which made DHL so successfully global, that DHL is a modern example of visible evolution in the way it continuously optimized the flow of goods throughout and across the globe. More on this later.

Change Agents

As the DHL culture emerged, based on the philosophy of decentralization, more loose than tight (except for brand and message), empowerment, mutual respect, trust and fun, some of the early country partners started to feel themselves out of synch with the corporate DHL. The arrival of greater business discipline, reporting and a shared responsibility to the network were not universally shared among the first breed of country partners. Many of them had been appointed as expatriate Americans in Asia, and some of them were people who had simply not gone home after Vietnam.[4] Conversely, the new breed of DHL manager, many of whom spread out from the Middle East when Bill split up the world into regions, found the independent agencies difficult to engage with. Effectively, this drifting apart *was* subtly transforming the old principal-to-principal relationships (equal partners), in substance if not in form, to the less equal principal-to-agency construct, where DHL began to set the rules and expect certain behaviors, in spite of not owning the business. And the operating agreement was not always supported by independent agents who regarded the outbound business as their own. Further, there was not the same enthusiasm for change and tackling the regulatory issues. Put simply, DHL was outgrowing its local partners in many countries.

The Middle East had taught DHL that if the environment dictated that a local partner was required, by law or by custom, then that partner needed to be a national, with a strong position and reputation, economically and politically. As a consequence, much of the 80s and early 90s saw varying degrees of turmoil, mainly in Southeast Asia, as agreements with local partners were renegotiated, or attempts were made to negotiate, before the ultimate sanction of a cancelled agreement. In that case, a new set-up was necessary, with a new set of partners appropriately inducted and incentivized into the DHL modus operandi. New Zealand was dealt with through straight acquisition, as there were no restrictions on foreign ownership. Indonesia, on the other hand, required one hundred percent local ownership of service businesses, so the first-generation American partner was on shaky ground from the outset. A new partner was identified, and a changeover occurred in less than orderly fashion. DHL used a tried and tested approach, bringing in a small army of expatriates to assist in the transition, and reassure customers that a stronger, more reliable service would result, which turned out to be the case.

Similar transitions took place in Malaysia and later in Thailand, but it was not universal that early partners couldn't keep up. The Philippines, with mixed local and American ownership, kept up with the DHL pace, and Korea remained locally owned by someone who saw the value of changing as his business partner changed and developed. The partnership in India was also successful and enduring.

These changing of the guards, which also occurred in the Middle East and Africa over the years, were not a repudiation of the partnership culture which DHL embraced as it expanded across the globe. Rather they were a strengthening or recalibration of relationships which augmented the reality of the DHL customer promise of control— "it never leaves our hands" was one tag line deployed

---

4 There was one striking exception, an American who started in Singapore, and enjoyed a long and successful career as Regional Director in Latin America.

during this period. And it was a clear signal to local partners that they had to keep up with the play, and actively contribute, economically and culturally.

Pirates of the Caribbean (Never Waste a Good Crisis)

In 1986, DHL's agent in the Caribbean, Island Couriers, who enjoyed an effective monopoly across the island nations, received an offer they couldn't refuse. FedEx's aggressive and well-priced offer to acquire them outright was predicated on giving DHL a bloody nose, by giving minimal notice of withdrawal of service. An early morning phone call to a senior manager announced that DHL had less than ninety days to find a way to service thousands of customers spread through over twenty islands.

But network expansion was a second nature and DHL promptly assembled an international task force. Eight markets in the Caribbean and Bermuda—which is technically not in the Caribbean—were identified. Senior DHL personnel were deployed for between three and six months to Bermuda, the Caymans, the Dutch West Indies, the British and US Virgin Islands, Barbados, the French West Indies, former island of Hispaniola (comprising Spanish-speaking Dominican Republic and French-speaking Haiti) and Jamaica.

Identifying local partners where required, company incorporation, premises leasing, regulatory compliance, customs and airline relationship building, local management recruitment, staff hiring and training, customer liaison and corporate image building were entrusted to the task force.

Agents initially appointed in the remaining smaller islands were progressively converted. Miami and New York consolidation points were expanded to improve services and transit times.

The challenges of successfully building a service network in a relatively small but multi-location, multilingual and multicultural developing market were overcome within the required time frame. Twelve months after the task force became operative, DHL's business to and from the Caribbean and Bermuda exceeded that prior to the Island Courier agency.

At the time, a few of the new managers in DHL often wondered if the original teams who built DHL had run out of steam and should be retired. But in this case, once again, they proved they still had the right stuff. Their passion and heart was on show for every single person in DHL, who could see in these individuals what the DHL service spirit was all about.

Expat Versus Local

The explosive growth which DHL enjoyed in the 80s was driven by a cadre of expatriates, ready to travel at a moment's notice, and fearless in the face of regulatory and other logistical barriers. They were a motley crew, some of them with university degrees, none of them with business degrees, but all of them infected by the DHL virus and ready and capable of spreading that virus into the many, many locals who were given not just employment but also an exciting introduction and insight into a world beyond their strictly local perspective. For the most part they were Anglo-Saxon, but, as Latin America came online, there were, for the first time, a smattering of U.S. Spanish-speaking expats, and increasingly in Africa, the Aussies, Kiwis and Brits were joined by French, Portuguese and Canadian citizens.

In Europe the expatriate also prevailed, with some Dutch and British exceptions. The Frankfurt hub was not staffed by Germans, and France was not run by a Frenchman; in fact, the early managers in both countries did not even speak French or German. This was fine, as long as the regulatory shadow lay heavy over the chances of survival. The expatriate could take the risk and just go home if it all fell through; conversely, DHL was and felt exposed when a dialogue commenced with the French and German post offices, and the DHL representatives had to be local lawyers who spoke the language and understood the political nuances, even if they were also somewhat skeptical about the chances of success. There had to be a point when DHL grew up, in the eyes of the local authorities and establishment, and appoint a local national who could join the business and industry associations and join in the broader economic debate as an integral part, an accepted participant, not a fly-by-night foreigner. Getting to this point was also a proxy for arrival and legitimacy, in that DHL could start to attract local talent who might in the start-up phase not be prepared to take the risk. The logic of replacing expatriates with local managers was also reinforced from a cost perspective: local hires didn't expect the frills of an expatriate, whose housing was typically provided as well as other benefits. But how could DHL be sure that a local hire, especially from outside the industry, could match the expatriate's knowledge, passion and aggression in the face of regulatory and other barriers?

This was a tension which played itself out over the years and is probably still being played out. What is the right balance between stability and being part of the local establishment, and the change agent advantage of the relative outsider? Steeped in the knowledge of how DHL works and what can be achieved elsewhere, the expat can bring a perspective which shifts the paradigm from "can't" to "can," from "why" to "why not?" One example of this tension was seen in the UK, a region by itself, and run by a maritime Englishman and his team. When the

Heathrow authorities set up the express handling facility, the local managers tended to think that the boat had been sufficiently rocked, and this was the best possible outcome. But the folks at MRI were just not happy with sharing the spoils with everyone else, and at a premium price. Why not push ahead for self-handling, and further disintermediate? This is what was eventually achieved, as it had been in Brussels, where the local authorities saw competitive advantage in attracting DHL to Zaventem Airport as its European hub. Pat Lupo's work on network organization, in Chapter 18, created a mechanism for working through these issues and potential conflicts, ensuring they were a positive rather than a negative tension in DHL's journey to full maturity. But more fundamental was a gradual move to separate the management of hubs and gateways away from the countries where they were located, to avoid any conflict of interest between making the country numbers and needing to invest in transfer operations.

Persistence at Heathrow, with Help from the US

After many years of courier bags clogging up the baggage hall, the British Airport Authority (BAA) approved the creation of an express courier facility on the cargo side of the airport, London Heathrow (LHR). The UK country management was happy with the Building 139 courier facility, itself the successful product of months of industry lobbying, but of course, that also threatened to lock DHL permanently into use of couriers and excess baggage for expedited recovery and transfers. The airlines were happy of course because they charged a lot more for courier baggage than for freight. The MRI team wanted more.

The simple-minded objective was to be able to use air freight mode instead of/as well as courier-accompanied baggage, but achieve recovery and transfer times in line with standard passenger baggage handling timings. An airside bonded facility was essential to expedite freight transfers and to allow for the planeside recovery and lodgement of freight, without getting entangled in airline freight shed handling protocols. All airside facilities in LHR were leased through the BAA to airlines only, and there were two airline freight groupings that monitored and ruled on all airside handling protocols. To add to the mix, all airline cargo handling in LHR was unionized.

It took about three years to get around and through all the vested interests involved—Gatwick, also BAA-operated, had a lot fewer entry barricades, and DHL was able to lease an airside facility there first, which served as a pilot to head off any airline concerns about the disruptions that might be caused at Heathrow.

Customs also had to bless the whole set up, and this was at a time when DHL's provision of advance information was still falling short of requirements. A concerted effort to improve achieved the desired results and soon DHL was doing more customs line entries than any other facility in LHR—HM Customs wound up using DHL as their poster child for other forwarders and airlines for volume, quality, and accuracy of entries.

Ultimately, it escalated into a union issue because all airside activity was traditionally a union preserve. BA, eventually the lone stand-out, held to the argument that as DHL staff were not unionized, they shouldn't be allowed airside as that would not be tolerated by the union.

One of DHL's long-serving trouble-shooter senior managers got the Head of the BA Cargo Handling Union to agree to visit New York with him to see how DHL actually worked in practice in a big airside environment. After several meetings with airlines and various regulatory bodies, the BA union crew were able to see for themselves how painlessly the DHL operation worked in practice, and began to warm to the notion of replicating this in Heathrow. On their return, they offered their support for the DHL initiative, which effectively meant that the last remaining BA objection had been taken out. BA management were a little taken aback at the tactics used to get their union heads on side with DHL, but agreed that the union objection argument was now out of play. The BAA then duly approved the first-ever lease of a Heathrow airside cargo facility to a non-airline, subject to DHL employing unionized staff for airside ramp work.

As freight movements replaced courier baggage, the airline spend at LHR reduced by roughly UKL twenty million a year, equivalent to taking twenty percent off the total international air spend at the time.

Chapter 17
Anecdotes, Accidents, and Altruism

In Chapter 8, there were a few vignettes which characterized and exemplified the emerging spirit and culture of DHL. Here are a few more stories, all true, and a closing story from Pat Lupo to introduce his contribution to this history in the following chapter.

Excellence Discovered

In Search of Excellence, by Peters and Waterman, attracted the attention of DHL leaders when it was released in 1982. Many of them thought that DHL ought to have been a case study. Shortly after the release, someone put together a training program based on the book, and released it for purchase. DHL Africa picked it up, and the senior leaders were trained to deliver the course to the various country staff scattered across the continent (of which there were many). Upon reaching Johannesburg one evening, the regional manager checked in to the hotel, and had an epiphany when he got into the elevator to his room. The little elevator boy was standing there smiling at him, and from his name tag, he could see that this little fellow was named Xcellence! He got down on his knees and exclaimed, "I've been looking for you everywhere."

Going the Extra Mile

In the same Peters and Waterman book there is an apocryphal story about exceptional service which has become folklore within Nordstrom, the U.S. chain of department stores. The story is not true, but that has never gotten in the way! Apparently one customer turned up at Nordstrom's with a set of car tires which wasn't satisfactory, and the sales assistant willingly took them back and got them changed, even though Nordstrom's doesn't sell tires! The DHL story, however, is true, and it also concerns tires. One night a Singapore courier was out doing a late delivery, when he was flagged down by a motorist with a flat tire. The man was an expatriate, and just new to town, and he had no idea how to go about getting his tire fixed. The courier radioed in to home base, explained the predicament, and base duly sent out a relief driver to complete the delivery, while the courier attended to the stranded motorist. He discovered that not one, but two tires were flat, and managed to get them both off and then to a local service station where

https://doi.org/10.1515/9781501507557-020

he refilled them with air. By this time the relief courier had completed the delivery and come back to help, so the two of them replaced the refilled tires, and the motorist was guided home, driving gently. The next day the DHL Regional Manager got a call of thanks from the motorist, who happened to be the newly arrived CEO of a major client.

Going Many Extra Miles

Couriers often went to great lengths to get their deliveries made or their consignments of green bags through. It didn't work out every time. One intrepid London courier, nicknamed "Biggles" after the equally intrepid aviation comic book hero, was stuck in Paris with the airport closed due to snow. He decided he needed to take a different tack, and loaded all the bags onto a train into central Paris, from where he took the train to Calais, making the overnight ferry into Dover. The next morning, he called the office at Heathrow to say he had made it, but still had the train to London and then Heathrow ahead of him. Unfortunately, by this time the flights were all operating again . . .

Making Calls was a Shoe-In

While DHL was investing in state-of-the-art fax and high-speed communications lines, down in Africa, it was still an ordeal to make any sort of phone call, let alone international. In Kinshasa, the capital of Zaire, one of the local staff had a friend in the PTT (Poste, Telegraph et Telephone) who had no shoes. He asked what color he liked and the deal was done. Hence, going forward every day at 9 a.m. precisely, the office received a call from the PTT asking where in the world they would like to call today.

The Green Bags must go Through

Another enterprising young African in a landlocked country further south was concerned because the green bag for that day's outbound consignments had no rope to tie the bag closed securely. A busy expat manager suggested he use his initiative and find something. The next morning, he was surprised to see the telex machine had been ripped out from the wall. The cables were at that time safely somewhere else in the world performing an essential task!

Shenanigans in Bahrain

Some of Bill Walden's incoming team had little experience in the big wide world beyond Australia. One soon-to-be senior manager on his global staff was initially based in Singapore, and was then called up to London for a job interview. The way to get there was as the daily courier between Singapore and London via Bahrain. One of the staff in Singapore warned him to be careful of anyone he saw in Bahrain airport wearing a headdress; they were sure to be secret service with a habit of pouncing on unsuspecting transit passengers. When the nervous courier disembarked for the one-hour transit stop in Bahrain, he was dismayed to see everyone wearing a headdress (part of the traditional Arab dress code in that part of the world). The poor fellow spent that hour in the bathroom.

The Future Sometimes Takes Longer

Satellite Express was the much heralded new product which would save DHL from the substitution threat of fax. FedEx had also launched Zap-mail, a service within the U.S. whereby documents could be presented at a street-front office, faxed to destination and then packaged and delivered. Satellite Express was DHL's global response. Both products failed dismally. It seemed that a normal fax followed by a fast courier was all that business needed, as opposed to a high cost electronic process with risks to confidentiality.

DHL Never Sleeps

One Sunday, the DHL manager in Hong Kong was trying to track an important shipment for a local client which had been delayed in delivery somewhere in Europe. As a last resort, he called the country manager in Europe and asked for his help, which was duly given, and the problem solved. But the European country manager also made it clear that he was not to be called on a weekend ever again. He was asked to leave shortly thereafter.

Never Fear, DHL is Here

DHL was asked to carry time-sensitive consignments way beyond the normal criteria of documents or small parcels of low commercial value. The list of novelties included:

- The replacement keel, weighing more than a ton, of the Australian America's Cup yacht from Sydney to New York
- A full size boxing ring, weighing four tons
- An eight-foot neon sign depicting Santa Claus in his sleigh
- 100 kilos of haggis, from Scotland to Kenya
- A crate of toilet paper from Australia to Shanghai
- Several tons of Berlin Wall
- Emergency G-Strings for the Chippendale Dancers
- An Indian curry meal from London to Moscow

Be Bold, Be Fearless, Be an Upstart

Ethiopia in the 1980s was embroiled in a long civil war which culminated in the ouster of President Mengistu and the formation of a new government keen on opening up trade and aid from the developed world to rebuild the nation. Business took off, but the incumbent agent was not interested in relinquishing control of the outbound service in favor of a partnership with DHL. An attempt to change agents resulted in the service being closed down due to political pressure from the incumbent agent. An approach to the minister of post and telecommunications resulted in an offer for the post office to take over the local service in partnership with DHL. This was not what DHL management was looking for as a solution, so they thanked the minister, asked for time to consider, and presented him with DHL's procedures manual to study, so that he was aware of what responsibilities would be expected of him in the event of a partnership. Approaches to all the foreign embassies and businesses gained support for DHL's preferred change of agent, but the way was still blocked. The DHL area manager decided to go straight to the top. Meeting the new president was not a matter of making an appointment; it required waiting day after day in the president's outer office with all the other supplicants for a glimpse of the president and potentially a chance to make one's case. After a week of sitting patiently, the DHL manager was suddenly given an audience, where he boldly explained to the president that the integrity of DHL's essential service depended on independence from local politics and political interference. There was no immediate answer, but a few days later the documents seized when the service was closed down were released, and the service was allowed to resume, under the new agent. The post office also returned the operating manuals. And the area manager, who started his career as a school teacher, pinched himself.

The Worm Turns

Conversely, by 1989, Vietnam was the last major country not serviced by DHL in Southeast Asia. Vietnam was slowly opening up, and the south was more liberal than the north. But it was still a communist country with a command and control mentality. This time the idea was to approach the post office as a potential partner rather than avoid it as the traditional adversary. Contact was made, and a delegation invited to Singapore to be wined and dined and made a fuss of. In Vietnam in those years, there was a singular absence of young adults in their twenties and thirties, just children and old functionaries who had served in the long war. There was a generation missing, lost, and so there was a dearth of commercial experience as well as people to do things. The deal, struck initially with the South Vietnam Post Office, reflected both their need and willingness to learn, as the service agreement allowed for DHL management. Thus, it was an emotional moment when the regional manager visited Ho Chi Minh City to see the DHL logo flying proudly inside the elegant French architecture of the South Vietnam Post Office!!

Unblocking the Funds

Bangladesh was one country where funds were building up because of exchange controls. The local authorities did not recognize the legitimacy of any transfer to pay for DHL's international costs of delivery for shipments originating in Bangladesh (net of any local costs of delivery for material coming in). In fact in the first few years of operating, DHL management deemed it impossible to even try. Some funds made their way out by way of a "loan" to the Catholic church in Dhaka, which was ultimately repaid by way of a check from the Vatican, less administration fees. Apparently, this worked a few times, as the church did not have sufficient local income to cover costs. But the new Singapore-based Southeast Asia Financial Controller, one of the original hires from Bill Walden's initial intake of professionals (who also happened to have played rugby with Dave in Sydney) thought this practice a bit on the risky side and determined to establish a legitimate process by way of the new operating agreements.

He engaged a local accounting firm aligned with one of the big global firms and made the case. The principal of that firm agreed and submitted a proposal for recognition of the network fee to the central bank. Twelve months passed. Funds accumulated. Maybe Bangladesh was in the "too hard basket" after all.

Another six months passed and the financial controller received an urgent message from the Bangladeshi accountant asking for help in obtaining medical treatment in Singapore. He was arriving the next day. Help was duly given, including the advance of funds to pay for the treatment, and the repaired fellow made his way gratefully back home.

Another six months passed and the financial controller received a phone call from Dhaka with good news and more good news. First, there had been a recent coup ousting the military dictatorship and a subsequent election. The accountant had been appointed as minister of finance. That was the first good news. Second good news was that he had just formally approved the DHL network agreement and payment of the piled-up invoices!

Thank Goodness for Unintended Consequences

Right at the start, when Larry was a fly-by-night courier between San Francisco and Honolulu, the folks at Pan Am were both intrigued and friendly. Staff, particularly airport staff, quickly became first name friends of DHL and its extraordinary people, and the courier processes were smooth and often generous (e.g. two bags charged for instead of three).

But later, as the regulatory battles with the CAB heated up, the relationship with Pan Am also became more confrontational (see Chapter 7).

As a tactical move, Larry and his legal advisors devised the approach of slowly accumulating shares, using scarce cash, with the avowed objective of getting Larry on the Pan Am Board. This was of course noticed by Pan Am's directors and advisors, and in due course good faith negotiations superseded litigation as the way to resolve issues. In the meantime, the share price kept going up as the airline industry enjoyed continued growth.

In the early 80s, however, DHL U.S. ran into severe cash flow problems and as a consequence fell behind in its statutory payroll taxes. This negligence could have proved disastrous, as the tax authorities had the power to summarily close the business entirely.

Fortunately, the Pan Am shares had doubled in price, the original tactical purpose for building a stake was no longer as relevant as saving the company, and so they were sold for a much-needed injection of what was effectively shareholder capital.

Unintended Consequences Version Two

DHL approached many banks for loans but were nearly always rejected because the banks wanted global audited accounts, profit and cash flow forecasts for the next five years, and assets for security. DHL did not own many assets and it took several years to generate the type of information requested by the banks. Further, banks found it difficult to understand the legal structure, with no head office and control apparently, but not officially, exercised by an obscure little consulting firm.

Larry Hillblom loved Micronesia and together with some other shareholders had squirrelled away some funds from DHL to buy Cocos Island (about one mile off Guam) and build a small resort hotel in the hope of getting a gambling license and generating additional income.

About the same time, the financial controller from Japan came up with an idea. It might be possible to borrow from a Japanese trading company using the Cocos Island asset as security.

Therefore, the shareholders agreed that Cocos Island could be used as security for the loan and after a physical inspection by the trading company and its bank, which coincided with the official opening of the resort and a conference of all the DHL Regional Managers and Shareholders, a loan of Yen 2,332,887,500 or approximately USD 20 million was approved.

The irony of this story is that the gambling license was never granted so the resort was underutilized until Larry and his co-shareholders leased the resort to Japan Airlines for twenty years. JAL sold charter flights to Japanese honeymooners to spend a week in Guam including a few days on tropical Cocos Island which was very popular. After a few years, a large typhoon destroyed the resort, but the lease agreement had a "make good" clause, so rather than JAL rebuilding the hotel they decided to pay out the lease in advance.

But the lasting impact of this seeming good fortune, was that DHL was able in time to repay the loan, and thereby established credibility for future bank loans.

Bill Walden's Office

When Bill Walden joined DHL his first location was Hong Kong. Po Chung showed him around the DHL office and proudly indicated the rather small office which he had identified for the new global CEO (in fact all offices in Hong Kong were and remain small). Bill thanked him courteously enough and asked if there was also a boardroom. Po showed him the boardroom. "Thanks very much," said Bill, "this will do nicely."

There was an element of posturing in this first move of Bill's: new CEO, big man, big job. But there was also an implicit calculation. When he set up MRI in London a couple of years later, once again he took the boardroom as his office, but only using it as a visitor would. After all, he was just the head honcho of a small consulting firm who travelled the world, working out of a suitcase, and, whenever he was home, he would also work from there (which was also true). This symbolic defense of the position of MRI in the DHL world was also played out by the entire MRI team in their meetings with external parties: the first ten minutes of any meeting were spent laboriously trying to explain what MRI did, without any pretense of being DHL's head office! Visitors' eyes often glazed over before the real business got under way.

Crazy Texans

In the 1980s, DHL USA would often fly couriers on multiple sectors between Houston and New York, during the night, with bags being picked up and dropped off along the way. The couriers learned to sleep in the seat upright position, so that they wouldn't be wakened by crew during landing and take-off. In New York, they would help with the airport sort, then adjourn to a bar for a few hours prior to making the homeward trip.

Negotiations in China

Dave Allen and Geoff Cruikshanks spent nearly two years negotiating a joint venture agreement with Sinotrans, the Chinese government-owned transport conglomerate. Dave's personality shone in this environment. Perennially cheerful, optimistic and at the right times self-effacing, he never gave up, and ultimately a deal was struck. Geoff remembers how the most basic of business conventions had to be explained and debated, because the Chinese officials at that time had little exposure to Western concepts of business governance. Meetings were long and prefaced by long speeches. Then in the evening there would always be huge banquets and multiple toasts of powerful liquors. Except that on the Chinese side, there were two teams, the negotiating team, and the drinking team. On the DHL side, there was one team of two people and an interpreter—who didn't drink!

Pat Lupo's Story: The Most Employee-Motivational Thing We Did

"Having completed and to an extent perfected the DHL footprint and integration of trucks and planes with the largest private telecommunications and computing network in more than 200 countries, which enabled us to instantaneously confirm the delivery of a shipment or provide real time information from DHL colleagues anywhere, we began to think about what uses we could put this unique neural network to. Neural, like a brain solving complex non-linear relationship questions like sending impulses where needed and marshalling resources to fight disease or repair a wound. A devastating earthquake in Mexico and a few years later in Turkey provided an answer. DHL teams in situ were able to send out handwritten messages from survivors as all telecommunications networks were shut down for weeks. And soon there was a follow-on cry for medicine and spare parts for generators, etc. DHL colleagues responded and worked around the clock.

Medecins sans Frontières (MSF) is an incredible organization which as its name implies, provides doctors and medicines in conflict zones and immediately following a natural disaster. They are immediately on call. Why couldn't we leverage the DHL network which could provide virtually anything anywhere in the world in 24–48 hours? So we contacted Jacques Pinel, the visionary and charismatic founder of MSF, and put at their disposal DHL's network of planes, trucks and telecommunications to move whatever needed to be transported on an on-call urgent basis.

I was a bit unsure whether this was pushing things too far to ask colleagues to divert their attention from mission critical customer deliveries to urgent medical supplies and spare parts (where the challenge could last months).

The DHL team members were amazing. Their can-do spirit responded in incredible ways to alleviate loss and Injury. Imagine the lives saved by having antibiotics, bandages, and clean water available in a matter of days versus weeks. They worked tirelessly securing medical supplies and small parts, loading aircraft and trucks and mobilizing our workforce to alleviate suffering.

Never before had I seen such a wellspring of team spirit. DHL people were so proud of their company, their colleagues and themselves in dedicating this incredible asset—the DHL network—to doctors and nurses. I made a promise to MSF: If there is a disaster anywhere in the world "all you have to do is call and we'll be there" (which at that time was the tag line from a DHL commercial as sung by Diana Ross). This promise to MSF gave DHL a whole new meaning and inspired colleagues like never before. When DHL people caught a glimpse of the DHL logo on a plane or truck or the shirt of a colleague, they said "it gave them goose bumps of pride and admiration that they worked for a company such as this."

Chapter 18
Adolescence to Adulthood

Mission Almost Accomplished

When Bill Walden retired, most of what he set out to achieve had in his own terms been accomplished. In simple terms there was structure, process and financial discipline. Respect for budgets. Tight controls in terms of what contributes to building a strong balance sheet and tight oversight on brand and image. Loose in almost every other respect. What had been cherished by the founders, in terms of people power, had been saved. DHL was a recognized global leader in its field and among its peers; the amorphous nature of the "mess with money" that he surveyed in 1979 had taken greater form. But not a traditional form—a network form—a different type of multinational, closer to that mythical rootless corporation guided by the market as opposed to allegiance to a particular home country, which Doremus, Keller, Pauly and Reich much later idealize, in their 1998 work already referenced. And it was not yet financially secure. DHL was making considerable investments in hard assets such as planes, automation, bigger vehicles and acquisitions, as well as more speculative investments into technologies and continuing expansion of the network. Revenues in 1986 fell short of the $1 billion mark which Bill had set out to achieve, but not by much, and still, a remarkable achievement. From $100 + million to over $900m in seven years was a good effort. But not enough to self-generate the capital required to exploit all opportunities and maintain market share. Nonetheless by 1986 the groundwork was largely laid, for more than three times that growth in revenues over the next decade.

A New Man in Charge

Pat Lupo was one of the young lawyers who worked with one of Larry's law professors, Pete Donnici, in San Francisco. He was therefore involved with DHL almost from the outset, certainly from the time the first regulatory battles surfaced with Loomis whistleblowing to the CAB. He became DHL's first corporate counsel almost as his first job. He became directly involved in the management of DHL when Bill Walden appointed two executives to deputize for him, with Pat being given responsibility for the Americas, and the other chap, an import from outside the industry, given the rest of the world. There were early signs that this latter appointment wasn't working out, so when Bill retired, Pat got the nod from Bill,

https://doi.org/10.1515/9781501507557-021

Larry and the other shareholders, and became Global CEO in 1986. Pat was thirty-five years old, and DHL was still broke.

Pat Lupo

Trained as a lawyer, with no previous business experience, Pat may have been considered an unlikely choice. However, he had been well prepared through working with Bill, and knew all the founders intimately because he was DHL's main legal counsel during all the years of regulatory struggle. And he knew Larry better than anyone, as well as being able to interpret and soften Larry's more strident nature and style, as the direction he set from afar was often translated by Pat into more palatable language as well as rationale. Finally he knew the DHL people, had grown up himself with them, and was also able to empathize with the philosophical underpinnings which Po was beginning to articulate as the bedrock of DHL's emerging culture and modus operandi.

He was also conscious of the fact that with Bill gone, there was a dearth of external experience in the top leadership. He saw his own role as finishing off Bill's work to get the company to investor-ready, such that access to capital could be achieved, and part of that process of guiding DHL from adolescence into adulthood was to bring in further expertise from the outside. One of his first moves, therefore, was to appoint his own successor to the role of managing the Americas, a man who had a proven track record in the food service industry. Subsequently he replaced his former colleague in charge of the rest of the world, and divided the world up into three super-regions, Asia, the Americas, and Europe and Africa.

This incidentally brought Po Chung back into the senior leadership group as the only founder with an executive role.

Bring in the Suits

The new Americas CEO convinced Pat that even more external expertise was both necessary and available, given the pressure DHL was under with FedEx moving quickly and aggressively internationally, and UPS also stirring. Enter Bain & Company, one of the "big three" global management consultancy companies which dominated the consulting industry at this time. Bain's approach was to dig deep into the data and examine the trends, ultimately tracking DHL's performance over time. Like many companies at that time, DHL was data rich, but information poor. And rather than follow the natural instincts of the aggressive but inexperienced young management team to grow faster through acquisition, Pat wanted to ensure that DHL was getting the most out of what it had already. So, the work with Bain & Co focused on understanding cost trends over time, looking at market and customer segments, market share, and comparing DHL's performance to best practice across many industries. There wasn't a lot of data on the express industry itself.

In August 1987, Pat called a special global meeting for all the regional managers in New York, not the most comfortable place to meet given New York's hot, steamy, humid summer climate. But the heat was on. FedEx was moving aggressively with its acquisition of Flying Tigers, its move into Europe (flying directly into Brussels), its aggressive move into the Caribbean (acquiring DHL's agent partner) and a host of other acquisitions. UPS was also beginning to move, and working with DHL in an effort to obtain flying rights into Japan, to counter FedEx's newly acquired rights via Flying Tigers. And TNT was looking at taking more of Airborne. The competitive landscape was changing rapidly as the industry globalized.

This was a watershed meeting, as over three days DHL's managers were treated to a strategy master-class in analysis arising from the Bain research, led by Mark Daniell and his team. Under the broad contextual theme of moving the business from operational to strategic excellence in order to reach its full potential, DHL's business was put under the microscope, using the latest analytical techniques. At the core was the growth-share matrix, incidentally created by the Boston Consulting Group, from which Bain & Co had broken away to become an independent rival. The growth share matrix plotted a business and its products into four quadrants based on their relative market share and growth rate. Businesses would fall into one of four quadrants, Stars, Question

Marks, Dogs and Cash Cows. Stars would have high market share relative to their near competitors in a fast-growing segment. Question marks would have low market share in a high growth market. Dogs would have low share in a mature, slow growth market, and therefore were either being kept as pets, or begged the question as to why they were being kept at all. Cash Cows were high-share businesses in a mature market, and therefore could continue to generate cash as long as market share remained stable. Designed essentially to enable effective management of a diverse portfolio, the growth share matrix, in the DHL context, was an approach to evaluate individual country performance, because for the most part, this was a single-product business. But it also threw into stark scrutiny the efforts to date in the U.S. domestic market, which sadly remained a pet dog for many years to come.

Then the techniques for maintaining star and cash cow status, and nursing question marks into stars were examined, based on greater knowledge of costs and how to get better efficiencies from the business by examining the unit cost curves to ensure that experience was producing lower costs.

Finally, the consultants discussed how to better leverage best practice across the network to learn from those markets which were stars or cash cows. And how to embed these findings and approaches into the annual planning and budgeting processes.

The timing and approach here was significant for four reasons. First and foremost, it was an education for DHL's young leaders, most of whom had never had the business training which the consultant's approach embodied. Second, the moves by FedEx and other competitors were clearly creating turbulence in the marketplace. Third, it was clear evidence that DHL, under its new leadership, was not sitting still and certainly not complacent in the face of what had been achieved so far. And fourth, because at the same time, in the same city, discussions were under way with UPS about a potential merger.

A Deal Made in Heaven, But

Ultimately UPS did not acquire DHL, but at the time there was considerable enthusiasm from both sides as the deal took shape. The two companies were already cooperating via a joint venture proposal to capture competitive flying rights into Japan in a bid to counter FedEx's leapfrog into international markets and their perceived advantage in purchasing Flying Tigers. Perceived in the sense that both the FedEx and UPS models were about controlling the air segment of the service chain, whereas DHL was happy to continue to support the commercial carriers as long as timing, cost and capacity were aligned with the DHL service promise. This of course continued to be the case on most sectors for many years to come, but DHL was also now in the airline business within the U.S. and in Europe, and so it was logical to not allow FedEx an unchallenged position on key sectors, and also logical for DHL to partner with a lesser competitor (in terms of relative market share!) rather than to go it alone.

One of the key things Pat and the DHL shareholders were focused on in a deal of this nature, which was effectively a takeover of DHL by UPS, was the future and wellbeing of the DHL leaders. They insisted that DHL senior managers be recognized for their efforts in getting DHL to a position of being so attractive to UPS, and were also convincing in their arguments that UPS would be silly to lose all the experience in these young but successful leaders. And the deal which was initially agreed upon did recognize this. But like many deals made in an atmosphere of mutual respect and enthusiasm by the deal makers, due diligence offers the opportunity for the skeptics to focus on risk. Many of the UPS senior executives, on looking at the deal from both a risk and internal culture perspective, saw problems with an influx of younger, international managers effectively running the new international UPS. And there were the objections of a more superficial nature, such as the arrangements with local partners in the Middle East and elsewhere, the fact that DHL accounts were not prepared according to U.S. accounting standards (which they were not required to be in the world outside the U.S.) and a number of niggling issues which all translated into risk, which was then represented as a drop in the offer price. Deal over!

Finally, A Head Office

It would have been a great deal, although fraught with the prospect of corporate culture clashes. When it failed, DHL leaders just shrugged their shoulders and got on with the job at hand. One of the issues that rankled, however, was the fact that DHL's "head office" wasn't a traditional corporate office but a management consultancy. Pat saw this as a barrier to future deals and a problem which could be fixed. Belgium offered incentives for companies willing to set up global coordinating offices, and so in 1988, MRI was closed down and Pat and his team moved to Brussels to set up DHL's first global headquarters, another signal and symbol of a coming of age.

Concurrently he tackled the two connected issues arising from his super-region structure and the recommendations from the Bain review of identifying and disseminating best practice. The risk was that the super-region construct (Americas, Europe and Asia) would foster disengagement or rivalry and therefore threaten the cohesion of the biggest asset, the network. Especially as the new hires in two of the top positions were new to the company and not engrained in or shaped by the global culture. Po, of course, as the super-regional manager for Asia, was the exception here.

Organizational Innovation

So, along with the new global headquarters came global steering groups, organized functionally, and comprising representatives from across the world, chosen for their experience and expertise. Initially there were two, the Operations Steering Group (OSG) and the Sales Steering Group (SSG). The priorities identified by this first iteration of global coordination were first, operational excellence, process and procedure, and second, a need to respond to customers wanting global deals, centrally negotiated and sometimes managed, to reflect their purchasing power as premium DHL customers. And a common theme and agenda item was the sharing of things that worked and were therefore candidates for global best practice. In such a way, Pat put structure behind strategic intent, and created a mechanism for fostering internal competition for the best ideas, yet another example of the self-learning nature of DHL, but this time, overt and explicit. Innovation could now be identified and managed in the context of enabling different things to be tried in different environments, and then harvested once identified as best practice. Strategy, structure and preservation of culture in one organizational stroke. Later an Information Technology Management Group was added, to reflect the criticality of information technology as a driver of efficiency as well as competitive advantage. And finally, there came a Human Resources Steering Group, reflecting DHL's growing maturity in managing its human capital and facilitating inter-regional transfers. The steering groups became more cross-functional over time, and reported into a Network Steering Committee, which was effectively DHL's operational board, comprised of the three super-regional managers, and Pat's senior staff officers from WHQ (World Headquarter).

An Ongoing Emphasis on Data Networks

Like Larry, Pat was very aware of the rapid developments in technology, both in terms of computing, but more importantly telecommunications. The early investments in leading, if not bleeding edge technologies and products such as word processing, x25 packet switching networks, the Unix operating systems, group 4 fax and Satellite Express may not all have paid off, but cumulatively over the years DHL developed both expertise and a conviction that electronic networks both supported the physical distribution network as well as threatened the core business through substitution. The growth in the package business demanded that a package of data preceded and followed the physical journey of the physical package. Data in advance, for customs clearance, data close behind, for tracking and tracing.

The collapse of the government monopolies accelerated the advance of faster and cheaper telecommunications, which in turn supported the emergence of the internet, which in turn enabled the logistics discipline to develop. For logistics, the flow of data was more important than the physical flow, because data provided knowledge, which provided competitive advantage in optimizing flow, what Bejan would see as a modern example of his constructal law in action.

DHL was an early example of a telecommunications-networked business. Data flowed, first in batches, following the store and forward methodologies earlier used for the telex arbitrage products, then increasingly in real time as the telecommunications networks provided bigger and faster pipelines. In fact, the DHL telecommunications and systems network, built painstakingly over many years of experimentation and investment, was world-leading and unique to the industry.

Pat encouraged his information technology people to innovate, which in turn attracted the right people, intrigued by this early example of a networked global business. The idea of DHL as a neural network described the aspirations of an inspired group of technologists. But where were the pipes? Where was the capacity to mirror the ubiquity of the physical airline networks which provided DHL with its physical distribution capability?

Fast forward just a few years into the 90s to answer that question. In 1992, British Telecom (now privatized) approached DHL with an offer to provide high speed links, trunk lines, connecting all the major cities and hubs. This was very welcome, but then came the problem of how to connect 200 tributary countries into the main trunk lines. The answer was SITA, a non-profit cooperative, owned by all the world's airlines, which had global networks in place for moving passenger data. In fact, SITA's X25 Unix based network was the world's biggest private telecommunications network. SITA was approached, and was immediately very keen to have a new paying customer with the geographical scope of DHL. But SITA's constitution required that access to its networks was for airlines only. So, with no doubt some appreciation of the irony, SITA recognized DHL as an airline, and a mutually beneficial business arrangement was concluded.

Concurrently, DHL was approaching the last mile with an electronic solution. Special computers, known as customer premise equipment, were being rolled out to large customers around the world, to enable customers to automate the shipment preparation process and keep track of expenditures. With the SITA arrangements in place, these processors could be linked into the communications infrastructure, giving customers access to two global networks, one physical, the other for data.

And a New Sense of Mission

Pat learned an early lesson when he actively supported the idea of a new product, an overnight letter, designed by his people at the center. He tried to introduce it in top-down fashion to the regions and countries. The new product failed to get the support of the countries, perhaps in part because of natural skepticism about anything to do with any centralized management direction. So, when it came to designing and articulating a mission statement, something which captured the aspirations, goals and beliefs of DHL everywhere, he was painstaking in his approach to building a consensus.

In Pat's own words:

> What is DHL? What do we stand for, what is our mission? What seems obvious today wasn't so in 1986; there was a tremendous divergence of opinion. DHL people throughout the network shared a common service ethic but it was unclear what were the company's ambitions, principles and goals. When I became CEO in March of 1986 I felt we had to understand the DNA of our company. So, we set about assembling colleagues from all levels in the workplace and asked a series of questions about their company.
>
> After some months, a number of truisms began to emerge. A number of fundamental beliefs, aspirations and goals--even a shared vision of the future--became evident. But It was painstakingly difficult to obtain global consensus.
>
> We spent weeks debating a few key words and principles particularly relating to decentralized management and service aspirations versus cost trade-offs. We put our common beliefs and aspirations down on paper, reflected and debated for another month, and then had it imprinted on blocks of granite and sent to all DHL countries, followed by numerous video communications to launch the mission statement as a unifying force in all the disparate DHL countries. The impact was astounding. There was not, of course, complete buy in; there never was in DHL. I came to realize this reflected a sense of pride and overriding importance of local pride, conviction, and strength rather than a rejection of the global. And this too found its way in the mission statement. Thereafter everything we did, said, and worked for, was derived from and confirmed by the mission statement. It really clarified who we were and who we aimed to be? The mission statement endures today in DHL some 30 years on.

So along with this corporate dressing up came a new mission statement, carefully crafted with input from across the global leadership teams. Pat was impressed by the outstanding response from the countries, the sense of pride, initiative and ownership which derived from debating, passionately, how to describe DHL's mission. It was a milestone in the DHL journey, a coming of age, and an inspiration for years to come as annual strategic plans were formulated.

WORLDWIDE MISSION STATEMENT

DHL will become the acknowledged global leader in the express delivery of documents and packages. Leadership will be achieved by establishing the industry standards of excellence for quality of service and by maintaining the lowest cost position relative to our service commitment in all markets of the world.

This was very interesting for two reasons: first, the use of the future tense "will become" recognized that leadership in "packages" was not yet achieved. The challenges of moving from a single, simple product base into the more complex world of goods with commercial value still existed, nearly ten years after the initial efforts into the Middle East. Second, the positioning on cost was a very clear output from the work Bain did on the cost experience curve. DHL's leadership position was not going to be one based on all the frills; leadership was going to be earned, but not through acquisition.

The mission statement continued with a list of strategies:

Achievement of the mission requires:

Absolute dedication to understanding and fulfilling our customers' needs with the appropriate mix of service, reliability, products and price for each customer.

An environment which rewards achievement, enthusiasm, and team spirit and which offers each person in DHL superior opportunities for personal development and growth.

A state of the art worldwide information network for customer billing, tracking, tracing and management information/communications.

Allocation of resources consistent with the recognition that we are one worldwide business.

A professional organization able to maintain local initiative and local decision making while working together within a centrally managed network.

The evolution of our business into new services, markets, or products will be completely driven by our single-minded commitment to anticipating and meeting changing needs of our customers.

After the "what" statement came the "how," and everything which has driven DHL so far was earmarked here: customer-centric, using leading technologies, astute use of scarce capital, the prominence of network, and a focus on people and organization to foster and sustain the culture.

And so, Pat Lupo dressed DHL up with a fashionable new headquarters, mission statement of intent and core business philosophy, and an organizational structure which reflected the uniqueness of DHL as a global corporation. He also actively promoted the small package business, now called Worldwide Package Express (WPX), encouraging investment in innovative services such as the return, repair or replace service for HP in Singapore. DHL was all dressed up, and, unlike the old idiom, this time there was some place to go.

In 1990, DHL came of age with a partnership with two of the world's largest airlines, representing two of the largest economies, ironically both "continental" in mindset, according to our definition. Japan Airlines (JAL) came first, with a proposal brokered by its corporate advisor, another Japanese trading conglomerate Nissho Iwai. At the last minute Lufthansa wanted in, and they were so keen they were willing to forgo their own due diligence process by simply using the work already done by JAL. The deal was done in two stages, and fully consummated two years later, a total 57 percent of DHL was now in large corporate hands, both a compliment and a recognition that DHL's journey from zero to global, from start-up to investor-ready, was now complete.

But there were still challenges to face; here are some key highlights to round out the story of the first twenty years:

FedEx Loses a Battle

In 1992, FedEx withdrew from Europe. The main reason was that ongoing losses from the ill-fated Zap-mail product (a version of DHL's equally ill-fated Satellite Express) within the U.S. drove shareholder pressure on management to close it down and, further, to curtail some of the international expansion effort. DHL was proving to be a very tough competitor in Europe, and FedEx was also losing money there, so the European operation closed. FedEx's main hub was in Paris, but they also had operations at Brussels and DHL promptly took these facilities over, to cope with the expected extra business. This was seen as a complete victory, and for the next three years DHL enjoyed forty to fifty percent annual growth rates. The little company that could still could. And the DHL people were still firing in the field!

With the Best Good Will in the World, it Didn't Work Out

The partnership with Japan Airlines and Lufthansa brought mixed results. The three parties, DHL, Lufthansa and Japan Airlines, all agreed to use each other's services as preferred providers with preferred rates, but in practice, this proved difficult to implement. Each party had existing commercial relationships to protect, and DHL didn't feature high enough in the airlines ranking of customers; nor could the airlines satisfy DHL's needs, even on the routes they commonly plied. Exhaustive efforts to seek out other synergies, for example in procurement and/or property ultimately did not amount to much. So, toward the end of the decade, the parties started to explore an amicable split. The one party which emerged to buy out all three parties' shares (Japan Airlines, Nissho Iwai and Lufthansa) was Germany's Deutsche Post, itself newly privatized and with a mandate to expand beyond its borders and enter the world of logistics.

The Ultimate Compliment

In 2002, Deutsche Post took complete control of DHL, adding it to its portfolio of airfreight forwarders. Subsequently Deutsche Post added a global logistics business, uniting all three activities (Express, Global Forwarding and Logistics) under the DHL brand. They also acquired heavily in domestic services, including an ill-fated takeover of Airborne in the U.S., a process effectively started by the early DHL leaders in the early 80s. This acquisition proved problematic, and in 2009, DHL Express had lost its mojo as a consequence of the global financial crisis, was losing money, and staff morale had plummeted. Deutsche Post courageously appointed an old DHL trooper, Ken Allen, to run the Express business, and he in turn called on the old pioneers to record on video, as part of the new induction program, what it was that constituted the "right stuff" of DHL from its early days. From there he built a global training and development program which is unprecedented in its reach. And he turned DHL Express around. The soft powers of the first two decades are little different from the values ensconced in today's program (as seen in Chapter 21), and testament to their durability. Building a successful global business based on soft powers can be done twice!

Chapter 19
Powers

From the beginning of this story, two objectives were emphasized: first to tell a story; second to offer a framework for others, based on a retrospective articulation of what was happening in DHL as it was building. Some of it was known and deliberate at the time; some of it was intuitive and describable only with the benefit of hindsight and language which was not always then in vogue; and some of it was environmental and a part of those times, to be ignored or leveraged. This framework may be described as "powers"; they do not constitute a recipe; rather they are ingredients which DHL dipped into, mixed up and presented as its own unique recipe for success. There are twelve of them which are the most important:

1. **The power of the idea whose time has come. Right time, right place and right environment.**

    San Francisco, Hong Kong, London. America, Asia, Europe. Larry, Po, Dave. Complementary time zones, common cultures, common legal frameworks, common language (different accents!). Easy places to do business. Not quite, perhaps, the global symmetry which links New York, London and Hong Kong (NyLonKong) as the world's great financial centers. But there is a time and place symmetry here which DHL symbolizes, in its source of founders and cities from which to launch a global enterprise, in this way, at this time in history. And San Francisco's climate was better, as well as being the breeding ground for the technology revolution.

    Victor Hugo once wrote, "you cannot resist an idea whose time has come."[1] At the time that DHL was founded until its adolescence, the world embarked on a period of globalization never seen before in terms of its inclusiveness. Psychologically the wounds of World War II were healing, led in the West by a conspicuous next generation of baby boomers and, in Asia, the imperatives of emulating the advances in Japan which stimulated the rise of the Tigers. Technological advances in transport and communications challenged the tyranny of distance. The information age was being conceived if not yet born, but the internet was definitely an embryo which a few visionaries could already scan. Thinking more positively about trade and national competitiveness meant that in a few countries the notion of supporting, in-

---

[1] Victor Hugo: *Histoire d'un Crime*, Calmann Levy, 1877.

https://doi.org/10.1515/9781501507557-022

stead of regulating, business took root. When it came to the competitive nature of countries, time became the essence, in terms of facilitating speed to market.

In the 70s and 80s we saw the emergence of just-in-time manufacturing, led by the Japanese and specifically Toyota, whereby the practice of keeping on-site just the inventory that was needed for the current work, meant that inventory could be lower and therefore factories could be smaller as well as more efficient. This also meant the processes of sourcing and distribution needed to become more real-time and less batch-oriented. Originally this process was confined within borders, but increasingly the process of sourcing, manufacturing and distribution was distributed across different countries where the most efficient process and lowest costs for a particular component could be found. Logistics as a complete discipline and a competitive differentiator was born in the 80s and came to age in the 90s with support from the internet.

So, in this context DHL arrived at the right time, with its low-tech, pre-internet, yet very fast system for delivery of time-sensitive information in physical form. And in the right place in terms of geographic positioning and global reach. And just in time to enable physical infrastructure to evolve as a precondition for today's world of e-commerce.

Maritime versus continental cultures were important in terms of predisposition to going global. This notion gains traction when three further dimensions are added to the mix: the rule of law versus rule by law, the blend or correlation of Anglosphere (in simple terms those countries who use English as a first language and who emerged from the British Empire) and Confucian values, and service versus manufacturing as a vocation.

The simple distinction of maritime versus continental in terms of either being surrounded by the sea versus fully or partially landlocked is not sufficient. Great Britain is clearly the model for maritime with its history of globalization and trade. Japan, on the other hand, is surrounded by sea but for most of its history has behaved as though landlocked (with one striking exception). And France, Holland, Portugal and Spain have been seafaring nations and explorers.

Add in the distinction between rule of law and rule by law that differentiates the English common and civil law framework from that Napoleonic Code which dominates Western Europe and of course other environments where statism rules supreme such as the former and current communist countries. In rule of law environments, the principle is that laws should govern a nation, as opposed to the nation being governed by arbitrary decisions of self-interested elites. Or, in less pejorative terms, rule of law environments use precedent and case law for common law, and parliamentary processes for civil law. Innocent until proven otherwise, versus guilty until proven otherwise, subject to peer review processes by an elected assembly. Bottom-up, versus top-down.

Other features of what is considered the Anglosphere environment, in addition to the rule of law, include the sanctity of contract (and its broader, less legal sister, covenant); trust, individualism and respect for political and cultural differences, or, put more simply, freedom. On their own, these features are far from exclusive, but as a combination, they add substance to the distinction between maritime and continental.

Confucian values can be summarized as *benevolence, righteousness, propriety* and *wisdom*, which upon closer inspection can correlate to, respectively, *rule of law, freedom, trust and individualism.*[2] It is these soft values which manifest themselves in the power of character described below.

Finally, put these ingredients together and it seems evident that the one environment, (maritime), is more predisposed to the service sector; and the other (continental) more disposed to the manufacturing sector. Hence the financial services sector globalized around London, New York and Hong Kong; the accounting and consulting sector have been dominated by UK and US firms; conversely, Germany and Japan have fostered global companies excelling in manufacturing.

Thus, the power of time and place which influenced the phenomena of DHL's emergence was further underpinned by the predisposition of those environments to supporting innovation in the service sector and being ready to regulate or deregulate to support. The most striking example is the relatively liberal approach to dealing with the challenges to the postal monopoly which we see in the commonwealth, Anglophone countries such as Canada, Australia, New Zealand and the United Kingdom.

And the blend of Anglosphere values with Asian family values (underpinned by Confucian philosophical principles) has been identified as a feature of DHL's unique culture.

---

2 Kingsley Smith: *The Hong Kong Advantage*, 2016 (unpublished).

2. The power of a universal product that works, has value, and first-mover advantage.

If a business wants to be successful globally, it's pretty fundamental that its product or service needs to have global application. And it's huge if it is first to market.

DHL's service and the products which emerged to package that service were valued everywhere. Every delivery became a sales opportunity. Most people who received, also sent. And the way DHL's service spread around the globe was in today's terms "viral"; growth in the network meant that service opportunities in terms of sector options grew exponentially. What DHL offered was simple, reliable and secure, and the consequences of this speed and reliability translated into both direct and indirect financial gains for customers, be it costs avoided or reduced, money made through faster access to funds, more time to polish the bid, or just increased productivity from the faster flow of information. Time was money.

The tactic employed was also novel and valued: total control, the principle of disintermediation, with the singular exception of the commercial carriers who were embraced as both a necessity and a virtue (often a one way embrace, of course). But the carrier, whether it be a plane, a truck or a high-speed communications link was just a commodity to be used in the overall service, and could vary from day to day. What didn't change was control over the first and last mile, and over time, control over the information flow; information which followed or preceded the physical flow, where knowledge of the status of an individual shipment could be translated into positive customer service, even in the event of service failure or delay. The information flows were built over time as technology and telecommunications improved and became cheaper.

The first and last mile, indeed last yard of the service chain was far more important than the relative time spent providing the entire service, and was understood as critical almost from day one by the founders and early leaders. In those precious few moments of pick-up and delivery, customer bonds were forged which were not easily broken. Plus, the last yards of the service could be a point of contention if care was not exercised to ensure first that the delivery or pick-up was made within the agreed timeframe, and second to ensure the right people in the customer organization were being reached. Many a time a shipment was lost or delayed after delivery was made because of faults within the customer's internal supply chain. A signed delivery receipt took care of where the responsibility lay. Those would-be competitors of DHL who subcontracted the tasks of pick-up and delivery, and didn't understand the significance of last-yard control, lost the competitive battle.

The principle here is to know and control the complete supply and service chain which underpins the product or service. A company doesn't have to own it all, but needs to control it, through information flows, through contract, and through partnerships.

There is nothing fundamentally new here, and DHL wasn't the only business to have such universal appeal for its products and services. But the way DHL did it was novel at the time, and the combination of appeal and value turned every customer into an extension of the salesforce. The phenomenon of word of mouth sales is also not new, but DHL enjoyed this benefit in spades.

Because DHL was first.

3. **The power of customer focus and alignment.**

DHL was an early example of total customer focus. In today's world, customer focus is regarded as a given, almost a commodity, to the extent that it is taken for granted, or paid lip service to. Sustaining a service mentality and an unremitting focus on the customer is an equal challenge to that of mastering it in the first place.

DHL responded to and followed its customers literally to the ends of the earth, wherever they were and whatever they needed. The shipping companies, the banks and the oil and oil service companies were the three key industry segments which supported and drove DHL to exponential expansion and explosive growth. Construction, advertising, insurance, government, technology, pharmaceutical and virtually all other sectors including NGOs, quickly added to the ubiquity of DHL's appeal.

Customer focus leading to customization is of course both a virtue and a trap. By customizing a service or service component for one customer or segment, such innovation can be reused or reshaped for other industries. But there is always a limit to how much customization and innovation a business can sustainably and profitably manage.

DHL managed to avoid the complexity trap in the early days by keeping its pricing and service options simple and few. But as time went on, service innovation, driven by customers and eagerly designed or promoted by an entrepreneurial workforce, meant increasing diversity and complexity, for example in pricing as well as packaging. The need to rationalize for computerization along with a strict set of branding guidelines took care of these particular challenges. But the expansion into packages and the development of global accounts added further complexity.

Initially, idiosyncratic innovation was informally and intuitively managed by the sheer force of commitment and enthusiasm of the DHL tribe. But as DHL began to understand and embrace logistics as a customer offering, its own internal logistics and the coherence of its supply chain was threatened. From a business theory perspective, the challenge was described at the time in terms of mass customization as opposed to the extreme disruption of the "market of one," i.e. every customer getting a unique service.

The organizational structures put in place by Pat Lupo to share and institutionalize best practice were designed to pre-empt the pressures of mass customization. But it would take a more structured approach to customer segmentation to maintain alignment of customer promise and expectation across the DHL internal culture and supply chain. Culture and structure alone were not enough, and toward the end of the period which this book describes, new disciplines for understanding, categorizing and segmenting the customer base became necessary.

4. The power of vision and mission.

Did Larry understand the importance of the environmental context outlined above? Did he deliberately set out to base his business in San Francisco, Hong Kong, London and then the Netherlands (that most hybrid of maritime and continental countries)? Did he anticipate the strength of the hybrid culture which would emerge? Did he know about the colonials in London wanting to be cowboys? No, for sure, on the soft powers, Larry got lucky. And in his choice of international partners, he also got lucky. Their backgrounds, their predispositions, their characters, paved the way for the advantages which DHL took from its environment as well as the ability to inspire and hire the right stuff for the mission at hand.

Larry's vision was powerful, unremitting, uncompromising, far reaching, sometimes short on detail, sometimes overly optimistic, and unequivocally mercenary. Larry wanted to make money. Certainly, the idea of changing the world and advancing the human race was not anathema; it was a satisfying consequence, but not an end in itself.

Others in DHL felt less mercenary. The other partners were ready to wait, up to twenty years, for any value event; they were having fun changing the world. And the early leaders of DHL, with an emotional, rather than financial, stake in the business they were entrusted to run, found themselves as part of a movement, on a global crusade. Go down through the ranks, and people everywhere, especially those in developing countries in Africa, Latin America and Asia, were caught up in the wonder of it all: young people with hitherto no geographical or cultural perspective beyond their village, their tribe, their city, their country, were enthralled at suddenly finding themselves communicating with people all over the world, and being recognized, as a name on a memo or a telex. That sense of wonder, sense of belonging to something bigger, sense of being transported emotionally while the documents went physically, created an enthusiasm which was felt by others, especially customers, using the service and looking at or into the DHL phenomenon. Mission certainly helped DHL's journey even though for the first twenty years, it was an unarticulated mission; it was felt rather than pronounced, demonstrated rather than sold.

And so, the first lesson about vision and mission is that it needs to mix the mercenary with the missionary. This doesn't mean that to succeed there must be a specific purpose, product or service to advance humankind; of course, it helps, but it is not a prerequisite. Rather, it is that the mission and vision need to be inspiring and meaningful to the employee base, as they become the ambassadors for the vision, and through their personal experiences and observable behaviors, personify the mission.

It also needs to be written down. Pat Lupo led the process of writing the first DHL Mission Statement in 1988/9. Every senior leader participated in the process, and it was set in stone, or rather encased in a transparent glass block. Every employee got a copy.

5. **The power of culture and shared values. Esprit de Corp.**
    The way things are done around here; the unique DNA. The soft power which differentiates a company from its competitors and makes it hard to beat.

    When Po Chung was asked in the late 80s and early 90s about DHL's culture and values, three things flowed off his tongue: they flowed because he knew it instinctively, and also because they were causal and consequential; they flowed logically:
    −   Strategic thinking at all levels
    −   Push and support decision making to the lowest possible level
    −   Tolerance for mistakes which are shared and learned from

    If you zero-base budget, and you get everyone involved in the process, and you respect the views of the front line people, in this case the couriers and customer service agents, and you delegate service differentiating decisions, two things emerge. First, there is ownership, which in turn begets responsibility and accountability. Second, there are mistakes, but honest mistakes, and the culture must be to share those mistakes to contribute to the learning organization. Every day's a school day.

Of course, this strategic framework didn't emerge as an articulated phenomenon until DHL was in its adolescence. Up until then, the predominant adhesive in a loose, unstructured world, was trust. Trust in each other, trust in absentia, trust with money, trust with customers, trust with authorities, trust that a decision made was made with the interest of the customer and company in mind. If the service is in jeopardy, seeking forgiveness is better than asking permission. Trust also begets trust, and the early leaders, as they felt trusted, in turn found it natural to delegate that trust.

To these specific points a whole range of more generic characteristics are added which might seem like motherhood and apple pie to today's reader: close to the customer; the customer pays the salaries; everyone sells; a "can do" mentality; persistence and determination; teamwork and mutual respect; personal ownership of the problem; everyone acts as if it were their own business (but it feels like our own business anyway!). Two points here: first these by now well-understood concepts were just being identified and discussed in the corporate mind set of the 80s. DHL was way out there in sensing, if not explicitly knowing, the various criteria which makes up a killer culture. And second, it is not just any old attribute on its own that matters, it's the unique blending of all the ingredients into a cultural recipe which matters; in this context DHL's culture and values also dip into and extract from all the other powers.

DHL's values were family values, traditional family values as well as Asian values, where the Confucian principles of benevolence, righteousness, propriety and wisdom are to be found, principles which surface in the 3 C's and other powers. It was an implicit link, intuitive in Asia under Po, and subtly assimilated elsewhere. The DHL family was like a tribe; and staff had to be careful not to let this family subsume their own. Many a patient DHL wife or partner complained about DHL as a mistress!

One other value which can more be accurately attributed in retrospect because people didn't talk about it in those days, and that is the value of corporate citizenship, the notion of obligations beyond those to shareholders and employees. The singular aspect here which has relevance today was that DHL paid taxes everywhere. The operating agreement between DHL, the network and DHL the local operator guaranteed the local entity a profit. Yes, the network had tax advantages through its Netherlands offshore incorporation, but it also took the profit risk away from the local entity and ensured tax was payable. DHL's early behavior in this regard could be regarded as exemplary.

Finally, there was a hard edge to the culture: if an employee left DHL, they didn't get to come back. It wouldn't be fair to those who stayed, if they changed their mind and wanted back in.

6. **The power of a service mind-set and positive psychology.**

Right at the beginning the service versus the manufacturing mind-set was discussed. Emotional versus rational. Qualitative versus quantitative. The magic moment when service occurs as an interaction between two people; unpredictable, infinite in its variety, subjective. Versus the predictable process of making something tangible; routine, predictable, disciplined. The service mindset emerged in the 70s and 80s, virtuous, aspirational, as opposed to servile. Dave's cowboys were artists, not scientists; they reveled in the subjective, and they disseminated that sense of wonder and belief in service as an end in itself, to their colleagues all over the world.

Positive psychology. This is a framework which didn't exist at the time the DHL story takes place. The discipline of psychology at this time was focused on a disease model, how to describe it, categorize it, devise protocols and treatments. How to make miserable people less miserable. In the twenty-first century, we see the discipline of psychology also turning attention to the science and art of understanding happiness, and how to make happy people happier. This work is based on the work of leading psychologists such as Seligman, who has developed a framework under the acronym PERMA:
– Positive Emotion
– Engagement
– Relationships
– Meaning
– Achievements

Successfully applying PERMA, or building an environment where it exists, creates "psychic income," which means creating an environment where morale is high, where people always want to come to work, where work is not only fun, it's also good for their well-being and happiness. Where service is a passion, not a duty or motivated by tips. Where the tips are psychic: customer satisfaction. This type of environment launches staff along the Maslow path to self-actualization. In short, a world where you get paid to have fun as well as be psychologically enriched. Businesses are struggling with this issue today under the terminology of absenteeism (people not feeling up to work and not coming) and presentism (people not feeling up to work but coming anyway). DHL didn't have those problems!

7. **The power of the 3cs—Character, Competence, Care (plus Collaboration).**
   These are the soft powers which contribute the most to the culture. They are like the DNA in biological terms which underpin the miracle of emergence.
   – **Character:** character encompasses integrity and ethics; it embodies trustworthiness to qualify for the trust; it means not having any repulsive traits, invoking the Anna Karenina principle where one bad apple can spoil an otherwise perfect bowl of fruit. Finally, it underpins that quality of leadership which means doing the right things with the right heart.
   – **Competence:** competence covers functional competence (can staff do their job) and leadership competence. Will people follow them? Do leaders and managers hire people who possess skill sets they don't have? Do they communicate well? Turn this around, and ask is the company competent? Will it survive? (DHL in its start-up days was fortunate to find a cadre of manager/ leaders who weren't asking that question). And finally, applying positive psychology, does the company think in terms of head count or "heart count"?

That leads to:
   – **Care:** care for the service, having a service mindset, feeling emotionally upset and personally responsible for service failure. Care for others, having empathy, and as appropriate, sympathy. Care for self, making sure staff cash in also on psychic income, and look after their health.

Character, competence, care. Like-minded people liking each other. These lead to a host of other Cs, the main one being:
   – **Collaboration:** One person picks up, someone else delivers. Someone they don't know, someone far away. That phenomena exists in every business, perhaps not with DHL's geographical scope, but everyone is a collaborator in the supply chain which is the business they are in. Working together, and reciprocally. Looking after each other, watching each other's back. Their failure is everyone's failure.

8. **The power of network and organized best practice.**
   DHL was a functioning network before it had a head office. And that head office was the head office that wasn't. It wasn't until 1988, almost twenty

years after it started, that DHL created a global headquarters, to portray an explicit maturity, a coming of age, in the face of market skepticism.

The point is that DHL thought in network terms from day one, unlike most multinationals who think primarily in their home country terms and then struggle to adapt with other cultures and practices. DHL always acted locally, and thought network, ultimately thought global, but network in the narrower sense of each customer promise. This predisposition drove the de-centralized management style, the predominantly loose properties of local autonomy and decision making. It also fostered the emergence of cohesion around the understanding that what was done locally had global impact, and what was done globally had local impact.

The fact that DHL had no dominant nationality meant that the network was the mothership, the unique selling proposition, the hard asset. The other soft powers leveraged the network to disseminate the DHL DNA across cultures and languages. The network became a united nations of service. It became a physical precursor and then counterpart to the communications network known as the internet.

These same principles applied to the development of DHL's own communications network. When the building of applications became decentralized and loose in the early 90s, what remained tight was the system and architecture for internal communications, so that the regions could always message (talk electronically to each other) from disparate processing platforms. The DHL communications network was unique in the sense of linking one company globally. No one was networked like the DHL network.

When Pat Lupo created the Global Headquarters in Brussels he also implemented an organizational design which was world class, in a view expressed by Mark Daniell in his 2004 book *Strategy*:[3]

Founding his organizational approach on a state of the art view of both the emerging principles of transnational organizational development from the latest academic research and proven practical experience, the resulting organizational structure and approach were truly world class.

One of the core objectives of the organizational design was to identify, capture and disseminate "best practice." In a network of over 200 countries, unobserved if not unmanaged innovation could lead to chaos; conversely putting structure around innovation enables different things to be tried in

---

3 Daniell, Mark. Strategy: *A Step by Step Approach to the Development and Presentation of World Class Business Strategy*, Palgrave Macmillan, 2004.

different places without overbearing constraint from the center. "Best Practice" observed and harvested internally supports the emergence of "next practice" ideas and innovations which leapfrog existing norms.

Finally fostering an organizational and people management environment which allows people to move or be moved internationally enables the local, versus expat, tension to be managed as a cultural norm, and supports the injection of new ideas or impetus into any "question mark" environment.

9. **The power of optimized flow.**

Small wins everywhere, every day, obstacles removed. Bejan's Constructal law states that everything, whether animate or inanimate, persists, or lives by continuously optimizing flow. It claims to unify the laws of biology and physics into one simple concept. It is a far-reaching hypothesis, elegant in its simplicity, and the purpose in referencing it is neither to prove nor defend, but more, assuming its acceptance, to associate what DHL has done and continues to do with loftier concepts, such as we have with emergence. Because the hypothesis is that DHL deserves such acclaim and such association.

In the narrative, from the very outset, DHL's intention was to speed things up, to save time and money, by improving the flow of time-sensitive documents and then urgent small packages, through busy buildings, busy streets, busy airports, busy-body customs, and to and from over 200 countries.

According to Bejan, flow isn't always smooth or symmetric or gradual. There is laminar flow and there is turbulence. An erupting volcano is turbulent; there is no natural path for lava. It has to find its own way. DHL was a turbulent force and had to find its own way at first. But even when established, it didn't stop—route optimization, airline partnerships, hubs, dedicated aircraft, data networks—all examples of continuous and often disruptive innovation which optimized flow.

The simple courier route is a good example. In the early days, a courier route was one directional, typically inbound deliveries in the morning, and outbound pick-ups in the afternoon, unless staff were in a far-flung city like Sydney where pick-ups were done in the morning and deliveries in the afternoon because of flight schedules. And as they got smarter at dealing with flight schedules which arrived mid-morning and departed early afternoon, they mixed up the pick-ups and deliveries a bit. But even then, the courier route could be designed on a piece of paper, and optimized on an adhoc basis by the courier to deal with urgent, one-off pick-ups or "specials" as they were then known. In the late 80s, the step costs of putting on an extra courier or route or aircraft were such that route design became a more rigorous discipline, informed by better data and predictive models.

Fast forward to today's more complex world where the rise of e-commerce has led to a rise in home deliveries. Back then, a home delivery was rare. But the more common they became, the more marginal, because if the consignee wasn't home and the delivery failed, the margin in the shipment was all but lost. The advantage of delivery density is absent in the home delivery segment. All sorts of new processes have been needed to cope with the business-to-consumer market and make it viable. Dynamic route optimization, which requires complex mathematical algorithms and global positioning systems are today emerging to make the courier route more optimized. Elegance is emerging as the impact of these new tools is presented in a visual format, with before and after representations of the new way to optimize. The delivery becomes a moving target, because the consignee or recipient tends to move, requiring inexorable, continuous improvements in the flow.

10. The power of partnership.

DHL's culture was also a culture of partnership, external as well as internal. There were partnerships in countries where regulations restricted service to their own national enterprises, and there were partnerships in the service chain—most notably the commercial carriers—the success of which waxed and waned over the years. But it was a key factor in building a defense against the big fully integrated competitors. This is worth re-emphasizing: DHL's unique corporate, nationless status was a distinct advantage in building a global network and culture. Conversely, it was a constraint when it came to "owning" the take-off and landing times of the aircraft carrying DHL's express cargo. FedEx and UPS had the support of their home country as they built their global network. DHL had none of that support. Instead DHL had to forge alliances wherever it went, and strategic partnerships in those countries which became major transfer hubs. Having a partnership strategy and culture was fundamental to making those alliances happen.

DHL also treated its local, country partnerships seriously; there was none of the lip service often seen when a corporation promises partnership and ends up acting as if the partnership was a subsidiary. Consultation was the rule, not the exception, and thus when a partnership broke up or was abandoned, it was not done before all avenues had been explored.

11. The power of brand.

Whether an explicit brand is built early or late in the path to globalization is not the question here. DHL's brand emerged late, almost as the icing on the cake of the service and the service culture. This is partially due to the absence of a direct correlation (DHL) to what was being done, partly because of the maturing of the industry description (from courier services, to Worldwide Express) partly because there was no money for promotional activity. Other paths might allow for an earlier investment in the context of a marketing plan which tries to leapfrog the word-of-mouth phenomena, perhaps because of competitive pressure. DHL didn't have the luxury.

What is important is how successfully the people become the brand, how well the brand values are visible or derivable from experience and observation of people's behavior, as well as the service experience. The brand needs to be a comprehensive package before it becomes the one soft power which can be monetized on the balance sheet. And, once it is there, shining on the balance sheet, continuous investment flows into the brand, and ubiquity becomes the objective.

12. The power of leadership.

The founders of DHL were a mix of personality, style and approach which in combination sent a powerful behavioral message to the early leaders. There was Larry, the visionary with a pathological approach typical of the true entrepreneur: relentless, demanding, tireless, winning the argument before it started, and not a natural people person. There was Dave, the charismatic salesman, inspiring his teammates to just get it done, just within the rules, playing to the referee and winning against the odds. And there was Po, the philosopher king, whose thoughtful, big picture, empathetic style reflected a blend of Asian family values with Anglo-Saxon inclusiveness, a maritime disposition within a Confucian context. Po and Dave also were naturally congenial which offset Larry's harder edge; not forgetting the early smooth-talking salesmanship of Adrian Dalsey who set the scene for being customer-centric before the term existed. Arguably the perfect businessman is in here, in the mix of these diverse characters' greatest hits.

All the founders and early leaders were couriers from the outset, then salesmen, then managers and then leaders, first by example and then by disposition. Managing to ensure things were done right; leading to ensure the right things were being done. Tom Peters talked about management by walking around; these guys were scampering around!

Then came Bill Walden, from the outside, but well inducted by Po. Bill, the "old man," smoothed out the rough edges of the start-up DHL, itself barely a teenager, by bringing in the wisdom of the experienced, and a focus on the hard values of budgetary discipline, cost awareness and cash flow. But he also started to turn DHL outward, to its market, to become a market-driven company rather than just operational. And he respected and protected the soft power that he could see offered so much by way of competitive advantage. In many ways Bill synthesized the leadership strengths of the other three founders. And Pat polished everything up for market scrutiny and potential investment.

There are many ways to define leadership and what constitutes a leader. The simple truth is that leaders are those who have followers. Leaders are claimed to be born rather than made. In DHL, leaders emerged, through a master/apprentice paradigm where what is learned through experience gets passed down, and also passed up, in a continuous virtuous circle: leadership from the front, "do as I do"; leadership from behind, as part of the team supporting each other and the leader at the front at that time for that purpose; and leadership from below, as the philosophy of owning the last mile and the last yard of the service cycle gave enormous respect to the pick-up and delivery functions, and the couriers performing them.

Instinctively and intuitively, DHL leaders understood cross-cultural as well as cross-functional leadership. They were comfortable—in fact thrived— on the challenge of motivating people from different cultures and beliefs; there was a common purpose, a common "what" in the context of a pick-up and delivery, but room for the how to adapt and be adapted. DHL leaders by definition needed to be great communicators, both verbally and emotionally, and these qualities were part of the four "c" construct.

DHL leadership took things personally: it was their job to make sure people were having fun, getting fulfillment, psychologically as well as materially; if people didn't want to come to work, the leader felt he or she had failed. They also took it personally in terms of self-leadership, the ability to self-assess and the discipline to do it often. This is one reason why annual appraisals didn't happen (i.e. weren't necessary) until the 90s.

And DHL leaders had been educated predominantly in the liberal arts disciplines. Mark Daniell in "Strategy" describes the quintessential network leader as a Renaissance Man or Woman: "In that more integrated role, the leader must operate at all times as a modern Renaissance Man (or Woman), mastering the arts, sciences and disciplines of his or her time and providing focused and practical guidance across all elements of a complex business world." Po Chung and Pat Lupo were definite qualifiers in the category of Renaissance leadership.

In terms of company and business leadership, Mark Daniell also concludes that, particularly in times of turbulence, the companies which navigate successfully are:

- Flexible, agile, willing and able to move fast
- Externally focused
- Thinking long-term, not short term
- Dissatisfied with the status quo

This description captured well the very positive and responsive culture of the company in the late 1980s, which helped to lay a foundation for the changes to come.

The last comment on leadership is a generic one: leaders need to be generous and a market leader needs to be generous in the context of its industry and its competition. A market leader who acts entirely selfishly ultimately shoots his own foot: on the one hand, developing and supporting an industry position on a given issue tends to support market growth. Market leaders should have the confidence they can take at least their share of that growth, if not more. On the other hand, competitors have long memories of behavior they perceive as arrogant and self-serving. Market leaders should look after their feet and be generous with their leadership, as DHL was in its regulatory battles.

Chapter 20
From Start-up to Upstart to the Most International Company in the World

DHL as an entrepreneurial success story is both unique and yet not so. An idea whose time has come is vigorously exploited by an uncompromising, visionary entrepreneur. That's not unique, there are many others like it. But DHL's recipe, its timing, its niche, its experiences and its outcome are unique; a biological emergence utilizing soft power to differentiate from its competitors and emulators. It was a natural but turbulent flow system which had to find its own way, an example of utilizing nature's ubiquitous design principles, and doing so from zero to global without external capital, while barely legal.

To recap, in the late 1970s and 1980s, advances in transport and communications made the world smaller and fostered an enthusiasm for international travel and business. A generation of young baby-boomers shrugged off the caution and conservatism of their war-weary parents and traveled, mixing with other cultures. The influences from those travels went home with them. Multiculturalism blossomed, whereby diversity of a given society's ethnic base began to be seen as a virtue, a way to break down barriers, to make the world a better, safer place. Concurrently, businesses began to think and act as multinationals, and countries rushed to deregulate protectionist policies which constrained their own companies who wanted to compete internationally.

The collapse of the Berlin Wall in 1989 and the subsequent collapse of the Soviet Union settled the question of capitalism versus communism. The question then became: what form of capitalism? The choice in those early, heady years when globalization became a force for good was between the stock-market driven jungle which was the United States, with its emphasis on meeting the quarterly numbers; or the oligopolistic variant found in Europe, with economic power concentrated in old-moneyed organizations whose power was constrained only by the solidarity principles embodied in the German guild movement of the nineteenth century; or finally the emerging Asian version with its blend of Confucianism and western principles, an emphasis on family values, and strong, if not fully democratic, governments encouraging, directing and driving economic growth, a new form of protectionism or intervention which still, however, believes in global trade.

The global financial crises in the late 1990s, and again in the late 2000s, showed first that the Asian economies had built in resilience, absent ten or twenty years before, which enabled them to recover more quickly. Strong government

https://doi.org/10.1515/9781501507557-023

action has overcome the potential third or fourth generation weakness of the traditional Asian family business. Second, the global financial industry was not playing its part in promoting the unwritten covenant that the benefits of globalization should trickle if not flow down through all strata of society. Thus we have a world today in which more and more people enjoy the freedom and ubiquity of physical travel, along with the instantly global and long-tail nature of information empowered by the internet, yet many feel disenchanted with free trade, immigration and global business and especially with the political institutions and processes which have promoted such these past thirty years. This is specifically so in those western countries which discern relative decline in the face of Asia's relative ascendancy. Much of the world's western citizenry is paradoxically disillusioned with globalization while enjoying its consumer benefits. They see big business as well as big government as parts of the same problem. How can business recapture the high ground?

The emergence of DHL in the 70s and 80s offers valuable lessons as to how globalization can be mastered from a practitioner perspective, how a business can think and act qualitatively as well as quantitatively to achieve commercial objectives without compromising basic human values—how to make one's cake and share it too.

DHL Leaders at Global Conference in London 1986. Bill Walden's last.

The people leading DHL in the 80s were fascinated by the Peters and Waterman book, *In Search of Excellence*. They thought that surely the book was about DHL, such was the resonance of the Peters and Waterman framework. But, of course, it wasn't, because DHL was hardly a household name. It had hardly graduated into the world of commercial sustainability; did not even get a Tom Peters reference. Hence this book is not about *that* framework, but it still holds up well as a reference point. The framework which DHL built, a mixture of accident and design, is comprised of several components, which coalesce into twelve groups, or "powers," reflecting the importance of soft powers as hidden assets essential to sustainable global competitive advantage. These powers can be seen in almost any academic outline of what constitutes success in today's global economy. But DHL created its own unique recipe for these ingredients starting nearly fifty years ago, and rejuvenated them into today's version when the going got tough in 2008.

We hope you enjoyed the story; and more, we hope that the powers that were, as seen within DHL, help you with your *powers to be*.

The relevance to today can be tested by setting out the following challenges as businesses contemplate their global position or ambition:
- Are you leveraging the right time-right place phenomena, or in other words are you reading/intuiting your current environment well?
- Do you have, or can you access, the institutional values and preconditions which have consistently, over time, generated global success?
- Do you have a universal product and first mover advantage?
- Are you systematically looking to optimize flow?
- Does your mission have social as well as economic value? Are you fighting the battles which ought to be won? In this context, the battles DHL won set the preconditions for the logistics revolution before the internet.
- Are you building your business bottom up? In this context decentralization; strategic planning at all levels; solidarity.
- Are you emphasizing soft values? In this context: culture, the 4Cs, Maslow, EQ and positive psychology.
- Are you institutionalizing what works? In this context: founder values, loose tight frameworks, harvesting best practice.
- Are you building leadership as a humbling experience? In this context, if you are a market or people leader, be generous, not mean. Help the industry cause, hire upward not downward.

- Are you building a brand which helps keep you in tune with your communities? In this context paying appropriate levels of tax as well as other direct forms of community engagement.
- Are you equipped for turbulent times? Are you agile, nimble, fast? Are you externally focused, thinking and acting long-term, and dissatisfied with your status quo?
- Are you organized to encourage relentless innovation and next practice?

We conclude our story with a sense of optimism about DHL, tinged with anxiety about the global economic world. Despite the current retrenchment with regard to free trade and globalization, we note that it has been companies, not countries who trade. Countries can set rules, but companies will trade often despite those rules. And of course, people will still trade and are increasingly doing so.

Can trade barriers stop the new wave of e-commerce which has changed the way people shop? We think not.

Can the relative ascendancy of the Asian East show generosity of leadership necessary to calm the nerves of those in the western economies, still with potential for growth, but in relative decline? We hope so.

DHL Express is arguably the most international company in the world. It is established in more than 220 countries. It communicates in 45 languages. By virtue of its unrivaled presence, and without the politics and regional biases that bind other organizations and affect their views, it understands how the world truly works. Despite the current global uncertainties, it should enjoy another fifty years. As long as DHL people keep firing in the field!

Chapter 21
Epilogue: The 2008–16 Reincarnation

We thought we had finished our story at the end of the last chapter. We went to visit DHL in Bonn, to show them what we had done. In doing so, we were invited to their summer party and so had an opportunity to talk to most of the managers and a great many employees. The next day we presented the book to a group of DHL executives. Everyone was asked to read it and comment. In the end, we found that they liked it and gave us great feedback and even more stories. It is clear that DHL today has the enthusiasm and drive that beat the odds back then and is doing the same today, but with the benefit and wisdom of those who came before. In that meeting with DHL executives an update chapter was suggested and agreed upon. We asked for help; for people to talk with to get the story right. We didn't know then what we know now, but we knew some of it as recounted in Chapter 18 when we pressed fast forward briefly describing what happened to DHL nearly twenty years on from our story. But we didn't know all. So, this final chapter is dedicated to what happened in times of turbulence, providing an update which links the emergence of DHL and the soft powers which fuelled its early success to the DHL Express of today. Here it is:

Market Growth

By 1990 DHL's global revenues had barely touched $US 2 billion. Market share was a different issue. In 1990 DHL's share of what is in today's terms described as the Time Definite International Express segment, was close to 50 percent. By 1996, with revenues of close to $US 4 billion, DHL's share had declined to forty-four percent, as the impact of FedEx and UPS on both market share and growth was starting to be felt. Reduced share, but maintaining clear leadership, in the face of persistent price competition and price bundling by the two U.S. giants eager to capture share into and out from the USA. By 2012 DHL Express revenues were hovering around €12 billion, as the disposal of loss-making domestic services (discussed below) took effect. Market share was now in the mid-thirties, but DHL was still the clear market leader. The story here is not about declining share; as the pioneer in a competitive market up against huge, well-capitalized competition, it was inevitable. It is more about the impact of all those hard yards DHL won in creating a market up to 1990, after which the competition then leveraged to grow the market for everyone. From an estimated $US4 billion in 1990, the International Time Definite Express market for documents and small parcels was by 2012 in excess of €30 billion!!

https://doi.org/10.1515/9781501507557-024

A Much and Long Desired Prize Becomes the Bogeyman

To briefly recap the intervening years: In 2001 and 2002 Deutsche Post fully acquired DHL, in two stages. In the next few years Deutsche Post made several other acquisitions in the freight forwarding and logistics sectors and rebranded the Group as Deutsche Post DHL, with ultimately four divisions: Deutsche Post (German Postal Services), DHL Express, DHL Global Forwarding, and DHL Supply Chain. By 2006, Deutsche Post DHL was a global colossus with turnover of €60 billion (sixty billion euros, which includes 9 billion from Financial Services, sold in 2009) a share price of €22.84, and profits of €3.9 billion.

DHL Express turned over €16.8 billion in 2005, driven in no small part by an extensive program of acquisitions to extend service capability beyond international to include domestic services in key markets. One of the pivotal acquisitions was that of Airborne in 2003 which, as already discussed, remained the number three domestic USA provider ever since that momentous decision taken by Bill Walden in 1983 to support the entry of DHL USA into the domestic market, in an effort to delay, if not prevent, the international expansion of FedEx and UPS. Management's intent in those days was to achieve a ten percent market share, which was judged both achievable and sufficient to "keep the big boys honest." An acquisition of Airborne was on every DHL USA CEO's agenda ever since, but it had not happened before Deutsche Post came along. And because of that DHL's share of the domestic market never surpassed eight percent, which ensured it remained an unprofitable, but still beloved, pet dog for all those years.

By 2008, however, it was clear that the acquisition of Airborne was not working. Integrating domestic and international services into a cohesive service offering was more difficult than anticipated. Losses were growing as the market also declined in the fast-moving global financial crisis. Everyone was hurting, and not just within the USA. Other pressures were being felt as well, such as the loss of Deutsche Post's domestic postal monopoly. That year, Frank Appel became CEO of the Deutsche Post Group, and Ken Allen was appointed as CEO of DHL USA, with a mandate to do what was necessary to turn the business around. Losses of $1–2 billion a year were clearly unsustainable. Frank and his US Express CEO took the previously unthinkable step of exiting the U.S. domestic business completely, to concentrate on international. Exiting other (but not all) domestic businesses elsewhere in the world followed in the ensuing years. But the U.S. business was the one which threatened not just the Express Division, but the entire Group.

The following year, Frank Appel took the further step of a break with the immediate past and appointed Ken as Global CEO for Express. Ken was a twenty-year DHL veteran, having joined DHL in the Middle East in 1985, long ago enough to recall the spirit of those times. This appointment was regarded by many as a courageous move, but they were challenging times. During 2008 Deutsche Post's share price had fallen nearly seventy percent to €7.18, on the back of Group losses of €1 billion. The Express Division lost €2 billion, on the back of the restructuring costs in the U.S. Eight years later, a slimmed down DHL Express Division produced a profit of €1.5 billion from turnover of €14. billion, helping Deutsche Post's share price to an all-time high, closing at €31.24 at year-end (other divisions also performing to expectations). How did this turnaround happen?

Somebody Press the Reset Button, Quickly

Ken Allen worked his way up in DHL by taking on every task asked of him and doing it. From that experience came the gut instinct that while strategy is important, execution is everything. And the secret to successful execution is focus. Focus on what's important and act like a market leader, which means explicitly providing better service, consistently, at a lower cost than the nearest competitor. Act like a leader, have a lower cost base, and focus on what's important, which means customer satisfaction first. From focus comes growth, and satisfied customers will always ask for more. But before growth, go for customer service and loyalty. Connect with the customer whether that customer is internal or external.

Ken Allen

DHL throughout its history has survived by its strong connections with customers as well as employees. It's cheaper to keep customers than replace them. Motivated employees stay committed. So, go back to basics, the basics of customer service and employee engagement and connect. In DHL Express' case, connect also with the wider Deutsche Post DHL Group, following Frank Appel's group-wide mandate to leverage the existing assets and make the most of the group capability. It meant focusing on a simple product segment which minimized any overlap with what the other divisions were doing. But first, connect with the DHL people and make them want to come to work every day and give their best. Based on what Ken had seen in his many and varied years in the field, his gut instinct was that *everyone* wants to do a good job if they are properly motivated. Providing an environment where everybody *can* do a good job, because they are motivated, trained and trusted, is the primary role of the leader. Focusing and connecting, acting like a market and people leader, concentrating on customers and customer delight, ensuring employee commitment and satisfaction, and leveraging the group assets provides profitable growth, and profitable growth provides for investment and persistence. Investment and persistence provide for a sustainable future. *Focus, Connect, Grow* became the mantra and from which was derived the strategy which was then well-executed. This is the simple answer to the question about how the turnaround happened.

Focus, Connect, Grow: Pressing the Button

Back to 2008 with Ken Allen taking the lead in the U.S., the decision was made first to restructure, then completely exit the U.S. domestic business by January 2009. Reduce the number of service centers from 412 to 103, because servicing the international customers could be achieved with a smaller footprint. Close the hubs, reduce the workforce by some 70 percent. That was tough enough. But the problem then loomed as to how to re-orient and motivate those who were left. The problem was twofold: first, the employee base had been focused on domestic services, and had little or no knowledge of international business and DHL's preeminent role in that global arena. Second, and consequently, the DHL U.S. folk didn't get to know the advantages and indeed responsibilities of market leadership. Delivering losses less than forecast was felt to be okay. And that is not to blame them as individuals; no, the situation was the problem. The same situation which led to that strategic disconnect, identified in an earlier chapter, between DHL USA and the rest of the DHL world in the mid-80s. There was also a leadership issue in that no one on the DHL USA Board had on the ground experience.

The response was twofold: first, call in the posse. As in the early days, when an existential battle erupted, a team of experienced international players was called together, on short notice, and once again were up to the challenge. That is, up to the challenge of energizing and leading a team of demotivated and disenfranchised employees, and not afraid of digging in deep, getting hands dirty, uncovering the devil in every detail. Showing by doing. Second, underpin the tactical response with something more tangible, and soon to be more strategic. Invest in the people, train them, teach them about the facts and figures of international business, and DHL's leading role in those markets. Uncover the mysteries of trade lanes, far flung geographies; educate as well as train. A crash course in what the first twenty years of DHL were about. Invest, invest, despite the bleeding, invest as though there is no tomorrow without it. And declare everyone a winner at the end of it. Certify them! The Certified International Specialist program emerged from those frantic days of retraining and re-orienting DHL USA to focus on international, to understand what their international customers valued from DHL's service, to focus on delighting those customers with irrational zeal, and doing so efficiently and effectively, with every day being a best day. DHL USA has returned to profitability and is growing again.

Barely a year later, Ken Allen was appointed CEO of DHL Express. DHL Express was in the doldrums, and still in shock over how the U.S. business had impacted the global business and drained the corporate psyche. Deutsche Post was big on employee welfare and corporate social responsibility. The key bottom lines of the group strategy which Frank Appel was rolling out were the aspirations to be the employer, provider and the investment of choice. In that context, the Employee Opinion Survey (EOS) became a key tool, applied rigorously and regularly throughout the Deutsche Post DHL world. The DHL Express EOS for 2009 showed an employee positive engagement score of fifty-nine percent, which implied that forty percent of the workforce were less than happy and potentially looking elsewhere.

Ken and his team, two of whom were, like Ken, veterans from the mid -80s, were convinced that the old DHL spirit had not been lost; rather it lay dormant under the blanket of negativity which covered not just the DHL world, but also reflected the global malaise in the wake of the global financial crisis. And they knew they had something potentially reusable or upgradeable in the Certified International Specialist program which was by now a key platform to reinvigorate the U.S. employees and inspire the recalibration of the business. But it needed context. The experiences the leadership team had been through in the prior few years provided one set of contexts; the ideas about strategy and execution, or rather how most strategies fail because of poor execution, provided another set of contexts. Finally, knowledge of the history of DHL, and the culture and values which drove the founders and pioneers to create one of the world's most international businesses provided a third context. In short, all the history, all the hard yards recently gained and all of the business education that Ken and his team had experienced and absorbed over the years from personal as well as external experience, all bubbled up quite quickly and clearly into what became known in shorthand as "The Focus Strategy," a renewal strategy to conquer and control the future of DHL Express while keeping an eye on the rear view mirror.

We Have a Strategic Plan: It's Called Doing Things

The Focus Strategy is short for Focus, Connect, Grow and it set the scene from 2009 to this day. *Focus* first, and execute, because strategies are just empty words without execution. Above all else, focus, in order to return to profit. How do you focus?

- Simplify the product: no more than 30 kg a package, no more than 300kg an individual customer shipment, time definite, door to door.
- Be experts and masters in customs clearance, and track and trace.
- Get out of domestic (mostly).
- Slash the overhead enemy, and cut costs. Make cost cutting, downsizing, product exits, not just acceptable, but sassy and sexy.

Costs disappear when quality rises. Quality rises if things are done right the first time. There is a natural and causal relationship between quality and lower relative cost (relative to a similar competitive service). People don't create costs, activities do. Make activities more efficient, and then do more with the same number of people. Reducing costs can be positioned in a positive light, especially if it is well choreographed and communicated.

The strategy might be to Focus, but the plan is centered around doing things, just getting things done. Guided by a simple framework, or pillars, that remain constant as the strategy develops over the years, and the connect and grow pieces are added. After all, there can be no talk of growth until the ship has been righted and the black ink flows.

The four pillars which dominate the planning process are:
- Motivated people
- Great service quality
- Loyal customers
- A profitable Network

Focus: The four pillars

Everyone in the organization, including the couriers, are expected to know these pillars and articulate why they are important. And their importance has been underpinned in the communications process with songs. Ken trumpets the four most important things in life: music, love, sport and logistics—and music is part of a choreographed communications process which clarifies as it simplifies and as it motivates:

"Ain't No Mountain High Enough" supports the first pillar, and has been a traditional DHL song since the first television advertisements in the early 80s.

"Love Sweet Love" underpins the attitude of customer service in producing great service quality.

"Simplicity" symbolizes the ease of use, simple product suite and back to basics approach which drives customer loyalty and repeat business.

And, "Wanna be a Billionaire" reflects the now attained aspiration to make the business profitable again.

As the business turned around, the primary focus moved from getting the basics right ("*building a profitable division*"), to getting close to customers ("*as one with customers*"), to once again talking about growth ("*growth through quality*"), but not at any cost.

Focus, Connect, Grow became the mantra from which was derived the strategy which was then well-executed. This is the simple answer to the question about how the turnaround happened. But there are five other factors which are apparent as drivers for the renewal of DHL Express over the past 10 years

Ubiquity

The Focus Strategy is everywhere in the organization. Just like the mission statement from 1988. Ken's office is a shrine to the strategy. On one wall, the entire Focus, Connect, Grow formula is busily emblazoned; on the ceiling is a kaleidoscope of big-name global brands representing the customer base whose loyalty underwrote renewal and recovery. And on the opposite wall are the superstars who provide inspiration to the DHL superstars at the front line: Lady Gaga ("you are all superstars"); Russell Crowe as the Gladiator ("what we do in life echoes in eternity"); Yoda ("Do, or do not…there is no try"); and the muppet character who introduces the Sell Sell Sell exhortation. Everywhere, ubiquitous, repetitive. Never underestimate the power of repetition!

Motivated People: The CIS story

As Ken and his team conceived and started to roll out the Focus Strategy, foremost on their minds was the EOS score of fifty-nine percent. The question asked itself: how can we take the U.S. Certified International Specialist (CIS) platform and make it global? Quickly? How can we reach every one of our 100,000 employees within twelve months?

As already mentioned, Ken and his team were convinced that the DHL spirit of old had not disappeared, but lay dormant. Ken and two of his senior team, Charlie Dobbie and John Pearson, had been there in the 80s. They remembered. There were others still with DHL who also remembered. And there were a couple of founders still around, and a bunch of other senior managers who had moved on, but still remembered. (In fact, no one who played a part in the start-up and upstart DHL ever leaves. Either they die, or the pay stops. But they never leave). So, Ken reached out to the pioneers, and commissioned a video of them as talking heads, describing what it was like to work for and create a global company in the 70s and 80s. This video became part of the induction process and introduction to CIS.

But more: it was clear that taking CIS global couldn't be done with purely internal resources. Experts were needed. Communications and marketing experts, motivational experts, instructional design experts, psychological experts, brand experts, translation experts. More than one agency. Some of them were already working in some capacity for DHL Express. But they had to re-apply and pitch for this most global of programs. They all got on the bus. First who, then what. The objective was to rebuild profit through an engaged workforce, such that every employee, the vast majority of whom were couriers, could describe the four pillars of the Focus Strategy: motivated people, great service quality, loyal customers, and profitable network. Underpinning the strategy, four attributes, or behaviors, for everyone to embrace: *speed, passion, can do,* and *right first time.*

And thus, the CIS program went global in 2010, DHL investing tens of millions, despite the losses. A two-day program (now five days). Something for everyone. Something to inspire the newbies and overcome the cynicism of some of the old hands. The power of positive psychology. On the educational side, ramping up expertise while keeping the culture and history alive. Delivered in forty-two languages. DHL aspiring to a higher cause, the cause of international trade facilitation--earned all those years ago by breaking down the barriers. Take a test. Pass the test. Be certified. Get your passport. Be a winner. Be a superstar of the international express business.

The Foundation CIS program was launched on a baseline of emotion, and then developed further to enhance the curriculum, with functional and then cross-functional content. The messages around iconography—singing, images, sports—not only helped Ken and the team to revive the culture, values and energies of the past, but they also allowed them to communicate complex strategy quickly, simply and meaningfully to the front line. But there was a grave risk that the program could founder because of a lack of leadership skills at the senior and country level. How do they harness the motivational impact and sustain it such that every day can be a best day? How do they engage the senior management teams to ensure a return on investment?

In 2012, in a watermark event in Shanghai, the Certified International Manager (CIM) program was launched, as part of the annual global management meeting. Turn senior managers into chief energy officers (everyone can be a CEO). Just like the team that turned the U.S. around. How to lead others, how to manage self. How to manage at peak performance. The power of positive psychology. The CIM concept was introduced at the meeting by one of the external designers, and then the facilitators were introduced, none other than Ken and his team, already trained and ready to go. Thus began a process of training the trainers, such that every country manager in the network nowadays spends several weeks delivering the program to their own and other management teams.

Where to from here?

Currently there is an effort to fill another gap, focusing on the 20,000 supervisors and team leaders to help them make the transition from doing stuff themselves to managing and supporting people who do stuff. It's called CIM, Supervisory Excellence. It's a two-year-long academy, where people graduate, enjoy the ceremony and wear the gown.

Apart from that, it is more of the same. Frank Appel has taken the program and introduced it across all the other Deutsche Post DHL Divisions, so it *is* transferable.

And the Guinness World Record people declined to give the CIS/CIM program recognition as the world's biggest, most extensive training program because there was nothing to compare it to. Guinness records appear to be relative, not absolute!

Sue Stoneman, from NKD, one of the program designers and implementers reckons the success of CIS can be attributed to five factors:

– The CEO and his deputies have been the energizer bunnies; the powerhouse behind it
– The innate belief that 100,000 employees all want to do a good job, because all human beings are remarkable
– Leadership from the top, then the power of trust
– The CIS process is integrated into every aspect of the employee life cycle
– Ubiquity (haven't we heard that word before?)[1]

The next phase is focused on digital. Everyone gets a tablet. Tour the virtual warehouse using your augmented reality headset. Be there. Learn about the experience and then live it.

Discipline, Process and the Power of Routine

One of the hallmarks of the Yellow DHL [2]today is the ubiquity of systems and standard processes. There are standard operating procedures for every stage in a package's journey. Unlike the days of old, when the *what* was more important

---

1 Roger Bowie phone interview with Sue Stoneman, CEO NKD Learning, August 2017.
2 Since Deutsche Post rebranded DHL in brilliant yellow and red, staff now use "yellow DHL" versus "white DHL" to distinguish between the new and the old DHL (which this book is predominantly about).

than the *how*. The need to run in operating mode in 2009 meant that consistency, day in, day out became the driver of quality, of efficiency, of a healthier bottom line. Glorify and sanctify the power of routine, the daily grind. Unless staff face the customer. Then they can and must release all their pent-up creativity to focus on customer delight. Insanely so.

Maybe Fred Smith, the FedEx CEO was right when, in the late 80s, he questioned DHL employees' capacity to keep "firing in the field." Just wrong on the timing. In 2009 DHL people were still firing, but nearly half of them were shooting blanks. Press the reset button, reload, aim, and then fire again, this time with pinpoint accuracy; every day a best day.

The White and Red DHL of our main story wasn't big on global discipline. Local discipline, yes, but sometimes that discipline was different country by country. It didn't matter so much when growth was freewheeling, and the dominant culture was free-spirited maritime. Just get it done!

But what Ken and his team have done is insist on a global set of disciplines which enable the marginal savings to be identified, achieved and accumulated. Boring? Not at all. Not with music, love and sports as background. In fact, what is evident here is arguably the synthesis that only a merger with Deutsche Post could realize: the perfect marriage between the free-spirited maritime service providers and the disciplined process-driven approach of the great continental manufacturers. A synthesis of the service and the manufacturing mind-sets. Cowboys and engineers.

However, discipline and routine do not shake hands with innovation. Innovation in the Yellow DHL world is evolutionary, not revolutionary. Stability is more important than disruption. Ingenuity is more important than innovation. Standardization is a virtue, but not slavishly so. Flexibility and ingenuity are encouraged to fix any problems early, to use imagination and creativity to delight a customer.

In their 1997 book *The Discipline of Market Leaders*[3] Michael Treacy and Fred Wiersma argue that companies must choose and excel at one of three competitive strategies, and be competent in the other two: operational excellence, customer intimacy, and product excellence. Being in the service industry by definition rules out the product excellence strategy, in that the products should be limited and simple, but delivered excellently. So either you choose operational excellence or customer intimacy. But why not both, cried out those who found the choice difficult? It depends on how you do it. DHL have managed to do both by combining a *rationally* driven operational excellence (discipline and procedure),

---

3 Michael Treacy and Fred Wiersma, *The Discipline of Market Leaders*, Addison-Wesley, 1995.

beneath a more *irrational* layer of customer intimacy, which includes the employee as an internal customer. DHL's vocabulary describes being insanely customer-centric and innately respectful of the front line. Customers are king, but employees are superstars.

Great Leadership

Despite all the hoopla, all the razzmatazz, the choreography behind the leadership messages and presentations, Ken and his team remain just members of the global team. Humble. Informal. On a first name basis (just like the old days). Ken is more like the lead singer of an average rock band than the CEO of one of the world's most international companies. Even his resume has him being described by others as "rough-hewn." Further, there is an iconoclastic, self-deprecating style to the senior leadership team persona when working with the troops. But it is also a "do as I do, not just as I say" style of leadership. The leaders model the behaviors they expect from their people: commercial, focused, and philosophical, twenty-first century renaissance men and women. Leaders that people want to follow.

Ubiquity again

The big yellow machine is now everywhere. Deutsche Post acquired DHL because of its global presence. When they went looking to acquire a solution which globalized their strengths in domestic postal and logistics services, one brand stood out. There was only one choice. It was DHL. And such a powerful brand already, that Deutsche Post the parent brand is now subsumed (except in Germany) by the overarching DHL logo across all divisions.

The DHL brand is now a key asset on the Deutsche Post balance sheet. The 2016 Annual Report quotes a range of valuations up to $US 5.7 billion, placing DHL in the world's seventy-five most-recognized brands. Not bad for Dalsey, Hillblom and Lynn. Also Dave Allen, Po Chung, Bill Walden, Pat Lupo. Not bad at all.

One of the reasons for the brand's recent strength is DHL's love of sport, as a corporate sponsor. The DHL logo stands out because of its yellowness wherever it is shown, be it football, motor racing (cars and cycles), surf lifesaving or rugby. And corporate recognition is broadening in scope with its fashion, television and Cirque Du Soleil sponsorships. Not to mention moving the the Rolling Stones' gear around. The brand presence follows investments in sponsorship or relationships which showcase DHL's ability to be a logistics partner, to move stuff. Think Logistics, think DPDHL, goes the tagline. Think ubiquity.

Results are the only True Sign of Excellence

In 2016 DHL Express produced an EBIT of €1.5 billion from a turnover of €14 billion. More than 10 percent. Best day ever! And remember the EOS engagement scores? In 2016, the engagement score was 86 percent. The active leadership score 85 percent. DHL is aiming for 90 percent in 2021.[4] Not yet satisfied with the status quo.

Going Global, Staying the Course: The Powers Revisited

In Chapter 19, twelve powers were identified as critical to DHL's journey from zero to global. From start-up to upstart to a global first in class. Powers that are critical to going global can be distinguished from those enduring powers which are essential to staying global. And there are some more current observations to be made, recognizing the changing nature of business and business processes over that period. Specifically powers 4,5 and 7 are now combined into one.

1. Not surprisingly, "the power of the idea whose time has come," which was essential to going global, is no longer relevant. The "regulatory battles" are no longer existential; the "home base," no longer important. DHL is global, it clearly has a German parent, but it has a unique global culture and identity. The English language is dominant, but CIS cannot be delivered to its full potential in a single language. No, it requires 42. The rule of law helped DHL overcome barriers, but the threat of discrimination from more authoritative, top down, unpredictable legal environments is minimized by ubiquity and familiarity; being part of the furniture of international trade. And DHL has synthesized the maritime and the continental mind-sets into a disciplined yet creative universal culture. Beyond nationality. Beyond skin.

2. The "power of a universal product that works" is still relevant. DHL Express was seduced by the prospect of dominating domestic as well as international segments. The nirvana of one-stop shopping. It didn't work. It wasn't valued everywhere. To an extent the brand proposition has now approached a one-

---

4 2017 scores are 88 and 87 respectively.

stop solution if one consolidates the DPDHL divisions. But don't forget that customers like choice, and freedom to choose. So, DHL Express slimmed down, simplified its product, strengthened its universality and focused on making it work.

3. The power of customer focus and alignment has been strengthened as a consequence of product simplification, positively affecting operational excellence and customer intimacy at the same time. Customer focus taken to a new level by removing any temptation to tinker with non-customer facing, routine processes, and reserving creative energy impulses to delighting customers. DHL employees are international experts in their customers' businesses. And careful segmentation of the customer base and their buying behaviors creates the perception of mass customization. Every major customer feels unique.

4. The powers of "vision and mission," "culture and shared values" and the power of the "3Cs, Character, Competence and Care." Three separate powers from the getting to global list are repackaged as one, when staying global is considered. Not to diminish them, more to enshrine them, *to emphasize that soft powers rule.*

    The Learning and Development framework in DHL Express today is the world's largest, most extensive, perhaps not the most expensive, but arguably the most effective, and certainly the most international, the most global framework of its kind. Its structured, orchestrated, choreographed, and soon to be digital. And it is transferable, as seen by virtue of the fact that Deutsche Post DHL has embraced it across the group. It reflects an integration of all the soft powers which define the corporate culture.

    In contrast, the power of vision and mission, the power of culture and values and the power of the "3 Cs" outlined in Chapter 19, and as evidenced in the White and Red years, were distinct. Overlapping, but distinct. Partly because they were intuitive, partly because they were ahead of their time. But largely because they were not then perceived as a structured and integrated cohesive movement, as found today.

    Soft powers rule because DHL has been successful not once but twice, on the same cultural foundations.

5. The power of a "service mindset" and "positive psychology." The service mindset is about serving customers, colleagues, company and community. Meeting people's psychological as well as material needs. Maslovian. Deutsche Post has added strength and commitment to its focus on serving the community. The learning and development frameworks have added structure and integration. DHL is reaping its psychic income.

6. The power of "network and organized best practice." The power of network is still very much at the core of Yellow and Red DHL. Think Global, Act Local, stay close to the customer, still apply. A country problem is a network problem is a global problem. And the converse is true: a global problem is a network problem is a country problem. All for one, and one for all. Today's network espouses decentralized execution, but with central planning. SOP. *Standard* operating procedures. By all means be flexible, and ingenious when things go wrong. But if it is done right the first time, things generally don't go wrong. Innovation, therefore, is not a priority in this world. Hence, organizing best practice to manage the pace of innovation is not a power that endures today as it was in 1990. Of course, there are innovations; the "net promoter approach" to measuring customer loyalty originated in India. But it is not a priority, it is not an objective, it is not a core strength. Stability, not disruption, is the modus operandi today.

7. The power of "optimized flow" endures. Every small improvement in efficiency, every reduction in noise through streamlined, standardized process and procedure added up to millions of repeated improvements, adding up to millions of euros saved. For example, reducing post-route courier steps from twenty to five saves forty-five minutes. Time is money.

8. The power of "partnership" is different today, even though no less important. In the 70s and 80s partnership was a core operating model. It helped expand the network quickly and enabled DHL to overcome restrictions against foreign ownership. DHL Express today owns all but a handful of country operations. Less than a handful. North Korea is one; Cuba is another. But partnerships still thrive, now mainly with customers as well as with commercial air carriers, both passenger and cargo. And included in that are sponsorships, public service, relief agencies and of course the CIS/CIM team as examples of a partnership philosophy.

9. The power of "brand" is even more important today. In the white and red days, it wasn't a main priority because brand investment was constrained by a lack of cash. But when investments were made they had a huge impact. Easy investments like vehicles, uniforms and packaging played the role of slow-mover; global television provided hockey stick results in raising brand recognition. In today's yellow and red world every tool is used, respected and if worthy, invested. Sponsorship and social responsibility add icing to the cake, beyond customers to communities. DHL is mainstream and ubiquitous, no longer niche. Deutsche Post has been both astute and impressive in taking the DHL brand and making it theirs. Hats off!

10. The power of "leadership" endures. The power and influence of the founders, early leaders and pioneers have been immortalized in the induction videos. The personal attributes of today's leaders echo those of the past. Informal, motivational, cross-cultural, respectful, dedicated to the company and the business. Entrepreneurial as opposed to having the traits of a true entrepreneur. More like Po and Dave than Larry. But there is one small, significant difference. The exigencies of recovery and discipline have required a more top-down approach than in the past, a more visible, active leadership, trusting and respecting the front line to follow procedure and do the right thing. To be ingenious rather than innovative. Embrace speed, can-do, passion, but do it right the first time please.

The powers which helped DHL go from start-up to global upstart have thus endured, with a single exception. But staying global has required additional powers, which were not evident in those early years.

Focus, Discipline and Routine

DHL Express has turned around from a catastrophic loss to a record gain, in eight eventful years, on the back of a focused and disciplined pursuit of routine. This was a business which needed repurposing, fresh leadership and focus. Focus, Connect, Grow. Companies shouldn't grow until they can do so profitably. They shouldn't let success divert them into peripheral opportunities.

In the early years, focus and discipline were not hallmarks. Creativity, chaos, energy, individual heroism, even desperation, were more the modus operandi. Ready, fire, aim (fire again). Keep on firing. Limitless energy and stamina were a substitute for structure. And it worked. Chaos versus order was an existential virtue.

But in the yellow and red world, routine rules, and is promoted as a virtue. Why waste precious energy in varying the SOP, when that energy is needed to be insanely customer centric? Conserve energy and creativity for the customer's sake. The main thing is to keep the main thing the main thing.

Synthesis

When Deutsche Post acquired DHL, they were starting their mission to be the world's number one logistics business. They were going global. Deutsche Post was buying a brand, a network and experience. They were also buying powers;

some they didn't recognize at first. DHL on the other hand, was looking for stability and capital. Staying power. A perfect fit. It took a while to realize how good a fit. It started to show in 2006, when the DHL brand was adopted by three of the four divisions. It started to gel in 2008 and 2009, when Frank Appel and Ken Allen came together in times of adversity, having worked together previously on various integration projects across the group. And today it shines as a synthesis of the previously contrasting, if not conflicting, cultures and mind-sets of maritime versus continental, service versus manufacturing, and free spirit versus discipline. Opposites attracting. A powerful mix.

Renewal

A company doesn't get to enjoy or experience the power of renewal unless it has a near-death experience after a period of success and confidence. The risk is that success and confidence leads to hubris, which then leads to a loss of discipline and the risk of failure. In that state, they have the choice of capitulation, or acceptance, leading to renewal. DHL white and red never had the luxury of hubris. DHL yellow arguably did. But DHL Express (yellow and red) did not succumb, did not capitulate.

And to put this in context, virtually all acquisitions and mergers take longer than expected, desired or planned, before reaping the envisioned benefits. There is a wealth of literature on this. Deutsche Post DHL's experience with DHL Express is no exception.

What is exceptional is the turnaround and renewal. Focus, discipline and cost leadership while simultaneously investing in the soft powers. It may not be rocket science, but not many businesses will spend €50 million on its people while losing twice that much. The science is not rocket, it's just hard and hard work; but the art, on the other hand, has been distinctive, unique, and soft.

At the end of Chapter 20, we asked some questions of an aspiring global entrant. Although those questions are less relevant to the "staying global" situation of the yellow and red DHL, test them out yourself, and see how they do. From our perspective, there are only two related concerns. The first is about innovation. Where in the current scenario is the next burst of disruptive innovation? Perhaps after 2020, signalled as a year of reflection. Related to this, how does e-commerce and B2C fit in with Express?

We don't need to speculate. We've finished our story. We've gone beyond our original scope. We've been able to test our hypotheses. And we remain confident *about the future for DHL. Thirty years ago, DHL was still searching for excellence. Now they can claim to have found it. **Excellence, simply delivered.***

In 2019, DHL will be fifty years old. It has earned its half-century. It deserves a chance for another fifty years.

Index